GREEN MAN

William Anderson

GREEN MAN

The Archetype of our Oneness with the Earth

Photography by
Clive Hicks

HARPERCOLLINS

London and San Francisco   1990

1 *halftitle.* A border of
Green Men from a
devotional work on the
ways to Heaven and to
Hell. Augsburg 1518.

2 *frontispiece. Sutton
Benger.* A Green Man on
the exterior of the
church.

Note: the foliate head
that appears on the title
page and the chapter
openings is from a book
by Erasmus, designed by
Hans Weiditz, Augsburg
1521.

GREEN MAN. First published in Great Britain in 1990 by HarperCollins Publishers,
8 Graften Street, London W1X 3LA, for HarperCollins Publishers Ltd: London,
Glasgow, Sydney, Auckland, Johannesburg.

Published in the United States of America by HarperSanFrancisco, a division of
HarperCollins Publishers, 10 East 53rd Street, New York, NY 10022, and in Canada
by HarperCollins Canada Ltd, Toronto.

Library of Congress Cataloging-in-Publication Data

Anderson, William,
  Green man: the archetype of our oneness with the earth/William
Anderson & Clive Hicks.
    P. cm.
  Includes bibliographical references and index.
  ISBN 0-06-250077-5 (cloth)   ISBN 0 06-250075-9 (pbk)
  1. Green Man (Tale) 2. Archetype (Psychology) 3. Christian art
and symbolism—Medieval, 500–1500. I. Hicks, Clive. II. Title
GR75.G64A64 1991.
398'.352—dc20.
                                                                    90–55342
                                                                    CIP

96 RRD(H) 10 9 8 7 6 5 4

Typeset by BP Integraphics Ltd, Bath, Avon
Printed in Great Britain by The Bath Press, Avon

Designed by Malcolm Harvey Young

3 *Le Mans*. The Green Man as a foliate mask supported by three angels, in an ambulatory chapel of the cathedral, *c.* 1240.

For Jennifer and Colleen

Time and again you found his trace,
Taught by the heart of gold to look;
To you the Green Man showed his face
For life wakes green and gold means grace
And all, through you, enhance this book.

From
W. A. and C. H.

Acknowledgements

Our chief debt is to Kathleen Basford who wrote the first book of the Green Man and to whom everyone investigating the subject must be grateful for her learning, her scholarly detective work, and her fine photographs. We owe many thanks to her and to Common Ground who now hold her archive of photographs for permission to reproduce seven of her photographs in this book. We must also acknowledge our debt to Angela King and Sue Clifford of Common Ground for their enthusiastic support. Special thanks are owed to an unknown friend: he was following on his motorbike the courier carrying a packet containing many of the photographs in this book to the designer. The pannier of the courier was open. Our friend saw the packet fall onto the road from the pannier. He rescued it and delivered it the next day.

We are grateful to the many clergy and vergers of cathedrals and churches who have helped us, especially Dr Peter Walker, former Bishop of Ely, Dr Alan Webster, former Dean of St Pauls, and Richard Eyre, Dean of Exeter. We wish to acknowledge our friends in the BBC, Julian Henriques, Jackie Moralee and John Silver of *Omnibus* and Martin Redfern of the BBC External Services, for stimulating and enjoyable associations. We thank Peter Galloway, Alan Godfrey and Robert Genge of ICI Polyurethanes for the photograph of the Green Man in Vladimir (9). We owe many debts to friends and correspondents, notably Fionn Morgan, Margaret Lyttelton, Jeffrey Gibian, Rupert Sheldrake and Jill Purce, Jane Clark, Alison Yiangou, Madeau Stewart and Suzanne Valadon. We thank Alan Caiger-Smith for permission to reproduce his dish on the cover and in the book, and Elisabeth Collins for permission to reproduce two works by her husband, the late Cecil Collins.

Of those directly involved in the making of the book we are grateful to our editors, Stratford Caldecott in London and John Loudon in California, for their constant encouragement, and to Ralph Hancock for his editing, Deborah Williams for her picture research, Leonora Clarke for her typing, Malcolm Harvey Young for his design, Leigh Hurlock for special help and Lawrie Law for looking after the book's production. This book marks our sixth collaboration together in some twelve years, and for much of that time we have been helped and guided by our agent John McLaughlin of Campbell, Thomson & McLaughlin, with much thought and care on his part.

We are also grateful to those who provided photographs and illustrations: the Mansell Collection, the Bridgeman Art Library, Werner Foreman Archive, the Swiss National Tourist Office, Nationalmuseet, Copenhagen, Alinari, and the estate of the late Anne Ross.

Our keenest-eyed helpers in the search for the Green Man have always been our wives Jennifer Anderson and Colleen Hicks who share the dedication.

W. A. owes a special debt to the Harold Hyam Wingate Foundation for making him a Wingate Scholar for research into the subject of creativity, some of the results of which have gone into this book.

W. A. and C. H.
Whitsuntide 1990

Contents

Prelude

The Jack in the Green has erupted from beside the sea. A tower of leaves about eight foot high surmounted by an open crown of flowers with a mask face disgorging vegetation, he is escorted by several Green Men. Their hair, flesh, clothes and adornments are all green. They are accompanied by a girl carrying a high spray of flowers: she is completely black and very comely. The Jack and his escort process through the streets of the town followed by sides of Morris dancers and clog dancers. The procession halts in a street while each of the sides dances in front of Jack. Every now and then, to the delight of the crowd, the Jack chases a girl and has to be restrained and chided by one of the Green Men. The crowd now follows the procession along the sea front and turns inland and up to the castle on the cliff above the town. There the Jack rests on a mound in the castle wood while the crowd eats, drinks and watches the continuous dancing. It is a splendid day with the sun shining down on the water beneath the castle heights, exactly right for the purpose of the ceremony: the release of the spirit of summer.

This happens in the last dance, for which the Jack descends from his mound and bobs up and down on the edge of a side of Morris dancers performing a stick dance. They crack their wooden swords together as they romp backwards and forwards and one of them has breath enough to shout 'This is the best of fun!' The dancers drive their wooden swords into the leaves of his covering. The crowd cheers and Jack in the Green falls over dead. One of the dancers recites a poem over him and we are all invited to take a leaf or flower from the Jack for luck.

The occasion impresses us with the sense that we have participated in a happy and necessary rite that requires annual repetition. What I have described is not an imaginary picture of the Middle Ages. It all happened at the beginning of May 1990 in Hastings, overlooking the English Channel.[1]

It is the New Year's Banquet at the court of King Arthur. Arthur and Guinevere are seated with their knights. The banquet is about to begin when a huge man rides into the hall. His skin is green, his hair and beard, reaching down to his elbows, are green, his clothes are green, embroidered with birds and butterflies, and even his horse is green. He bears in one hand a holly bush and in the other an axe of green steel hung with green tassels. He glitters with green jewels, and in and out of his accoutrements and those of his horse run shining streaks and filaments of gold. He is the Green Knight.

The Green Knight rides up to the King and issues his challenge. It is that any knight at Camelot may strike his head from his shoulders provided that

4 The Jack in the Green with an attendant Green Man at Hastings Castle.

in one year's time he searches out the Green Knight to submit himself to the same trial. There is an appalled silence. Then Arthur, to save the honour of his court, takes up the challenge; but his nephew Gawaine begs to be allowed to act in his stead. The Green Knight accepts Gawaine as his challenger. He kneels for the blow, pulling his hair away from his neck. Gawaine decapitates him with one stroke. The head rolls away and blood gushes out. The body of the Green Knight rises, picks up his head, mounts his horse, and holds his head towards Gawaine. The head with open eyes bids Gawaine find him again at the Green Chapel in twelve months' time. 'Come,' the head says, 'or be known as a coward.' Sparks fly from the horse's hooves as he gallops from the hall.

5 *opposite. King's Nympton.* The oak leaf face of a Green Man on the rood screen of the parish church.

You branch off from the valley of the Taw in North Devon up a steep, narrow road through woods and hangers, winding up until you reach the hilltop village of King's Nympton. Passing the village pub, which is called the Grove Inn, and many old thatched cottages, you enter the churchyard surrounded by trees and full of ancient yews. The recent storms have felled some of the trees and so opened up a vista of receding forested hills darkening into deep blues and then growing lighter in tone as the summits merge into the horizon. The very exterior of the church arouses excitement, with its squat Norman tower topped by a pretty spire and its deep traceried windows. It looks like that rare wonder, a church no rough restorer has ever improved, and this impression is borne out by the smell of ancientness, the stillness of undisturbed stone and wood, the sense of memory in the atmosphere. The church is divided by a dark wooden rood screen carved in about 1480 and on it you see among carvings of foliage the head of a young man with wide eyes, and with oak leaves pouring out of his mouth and on the crown of his head. Then, looking up, you see bigger Green Men in the bosses of the roof of the nave, snarling, grim, sighing, watching, as though they were the guardians of the beauty and the power of the landscape you have passed through to visit them. And these Green Men are only a sprinkling of the thousands of their fellows who were carved in the churches of Europe long before and after their date throughout Western and Central Europe.

This is the story of the Green Man of Knowledge.[2] Jack, the story's hero, has spent all his life lazing by the fire and playing cards with his collie dog. His mother tends the farm and the pigs. On his twenty-first birthday he ups and leaves for the Land of Enchantment where all creatures and things can talk. Everyone knows his name and has been expecting him. Guided by a robin he is sheltered by an ancient woman who feeds him and gives him a piece of gold. He comes to an inn where three men are playing cards. One of them is entirely green. He is the Green Man of Knowledge. Jack asks to play cards but the Green Man of Knowledge will only let him play if he has money. Jack has the gold piece and he plays all night against the Green Man and defeats him. Jack is now rich but he is fascinated by the Green Man who, when asked where he lives, says 'East of the Moon and West of the Stars'. He leaves Jack who is eager to meet him again despite all warnings that it will lead to his death. Jack sets out and meets a woman even older than the first who gives him a magic piece of knitting on which he has to sit crosslegged without looking behind him. He flies through hail and fire to land beside a smithy where a yet more ancient woman again helps him and tells him to speak to the smith. The smith warns him of all the dangers and how he has to surmount them. He has to capture the youngest of the three daughters of the Green Man of Knowledge and gain her help. The smith then gives him a horseshoe on which he has to travel as he did on the piece of knitting. He lands beside a river with a bridge leading to the Green Man's castle. If he steps on the bridge it will turn to a spider's web; his only way to cross the river is to follow the smith's directions, so he hides and watches the three daughters come to bathe. The two eldest turn into black swans and the youngest turns into a white swan. Jack seizes the clothes of the youngest daughter and will not give them back until she carries him across the water. She does carry him across and then tells him that he has 'spelled' her: she will love him until the day she dies and she will help him against her father but he must never reveal that she is helping him. Jack goes up to the castle where the Green Man is surprised to see him. He asks Jack to prove he is a man by carrying out three simple tasks. The tasks are in fact impossible. They are: to find a ring in a deep well; to build a castle in sixty minutes; and to clear a wood of ants in half-an-hour. With the secret help of the youngest daughter all these tasks are performed and the Green Man rewards Jack with gold and offers him a mare from his stable. Jack refuses the two fine mares and chooses a mule to ride home on. The mule is in fact the youngest daughter who, as she bears him home, warns that the Green Man and her family will pursue and destroy them. Sure enough the Green Man chases them. Twice he nearly catches them and twice Jack, instructed by the mule, makes a spell that gains them respite. The first spell puts rivers, lakes and seas between them and the Green Man; the second spell puts mountains, hills and dales between them. Still the Green Man comes after them and with a third spell Jack sets fire, hell and pits behind them which destroy the Green Man and his family. The youngest daughter now resumes her human form and tells him that, for what she has done in destroying her family, they must part for a year and in that time he must not kiss or be kissed by any creature. She leaves and he finds himself close to home. On entering the house he avoids his mother's kiss but the collie dog leaps up and licks him. From that moment he forgets everything including his love for the youngest daughter. He is now rich and successful. After the passing of a year he is about to marry the miller's daughter. A beggar girl comes to ask for work and Jack allows her to help over the period of the wedding. She is, of course, the youngest daughter. She amuses the wedding guests while they wait for the preacher by making a wooden hen and cock talk together. 'Do you remember me, Jack?' asks the hen. 'No' says the cock. 'Do you remember the Green Man of Knowledge?' she asks. Again the cock says no. 'Do you remember me, the woman you love?' Again the cock says no. 'Jack, do you remember when I killed my own people for you?' Then the cock says 'Yes, I do remember you.' Jack then recognizes her; the wedding is cancelled and he marries the youngest daughter and lives happily ever after.

It is 17 August 1591. Queen Elizabeth is being entertained by Lord Montague at Cowdray Park in Sussex. After dinner, while being shown his lordship's walks, she is met by a Pilgrim with silver scallop shells in his hat. The Pilgrim tells her of a marvellous oak he has found. It is guarded by a wild ruffian and a lady called Peace. He begs the Queen to accompany him to the oak, which she finds to be hung all over with the royal coat of arms and the escutcheons of the great families of Sussex. The ruffian turns out to be a wild man 'cladde in Ivie' who addresses a speech to her. This oak, he says, exemplifies her strength and happiness through the loyalty of all the families represented in the escutcheons. They may differ in degree but not in duty: 'the greatness of the branches, not the greenness'. It is a long and very loaded speech: Lord Montague, like many of the gentlemen represented in the oak, is a Catholic. It is six years since he was removed from the lieutenancy of the county. It is three years after the Spanish Armada. Montague and his friends through the mouth of the ivy-clad man are asserting both their strength and their loyalty. The Queen listens graciously and is then entertained by a song, after which she goes hunting.[3]

     ⁊   ⁊   ⁊

I have been working on the Green Man for some time. I am fascinated by the way he comes and goes in the course of history. I come to a break in my work as I realize that a batch of poems is waiting to be written. There is one poem that is announcing itself as a rhythm of faceted vowels twisting and jetting through convoluted pipes and culverts of consonants. The rhythm haunts me over a fortnight or so and then it begins to attract images and memories of different kinds of trees. I come to realize that the rhythm is coming from the Green Man and that he is speaking through the trees at different times of the year.[4] After the appearance of this poem I realize that I have to write a book — this one — about the Green Man.

The Green Man

Like antlers, like veins of the brain the birches
Mark patterns of mind on the red winter sky;
'I am thought of all plants,' says the Green Man,
'I am thought of all plants,' says he.

The hungry birds harry the last berries of rowan
But white is her bark in the darkness of rain;
'I rise with the sap,' says the Green Man,
'I rise with the sap,' says he.

The ashes are clashing their boughs like sword-dancers,
Their black buds are tracing wild faces in the clouds;
'I come with the wind,' says the Green Man,
'I come with the wind,' says he.

The alders are rattling as though ready for battle
Guarding the grove where she waits for her lover;
'I burn with desire,' says the Green Man,
'I burn with desire,' says he.

In and out of the yellowing wands of the willow
The pollen-bright bees are plundering the catkins;
'I am honey of love,' says the Green Man,
'I am honey of love,' says he.

The hedges of quick are thick with may blossom
As the dancers advance on the leaf-covered King;
'It's off with my head,' says the Green Man,
'It's off with my head,' says he.

Green Man becomes grown man in flames of the oak
As its crown forms his mask and its leafage his features;
'I speak through the oak,' says the Green Man,
'I speak through the oak,' says he.

The holly is flowering as hayfields are rolling
Their gleaming long grasses like waves of the sea;
'I shine with the sun,' says the Green Man,
'I shine with the sun,' says he.

The hazels are rocking the cups of their nuts
As the harvesters shout when the last sheaf is cut;
'I swim with the salmon,' says the Green Man,
'I swim with the salmon,' says he.

The globes of the grapes are robing with bloom
Like the hazes of autumn, like the Milky Way's stardust;
'I am crushed for your drink,' says the Green Man,
'I am crushed for your drink,' says he.

The aspen drops silver of leaves on earth's salver
And the poplars shed gold on the young ivy flowerheads;
'I have paid for your pleasure,' says the Green Man,
'I have paid for your pleasure,' says he.

The reedbeds are flanking in silence the islands
Where meditates Wisdom as she waits and waits;
'I have kept her secret,' says the Green Man,
'I have kept her secret,' says he.

The bark of the elder makes whistles for children
To call to the deer as they rove over the snow;
'I am born in the dark,' says the Green Man,
'I am born in the dark,' says he.

Chapter 1

The Hunt for the Green Man

The Green Man signifies irrepressible life. Once he has come into your awareness, you will find him speaking to you wherever you go. He is an image from the depths of prehistory: he appears and seems to die and then comes again after long forgettings at many periods in the past two thousand years. In his origins he is much older than our Christian era. In all his appearances he is an image of renewal and rebirth, and it is my aim in this book to show that his reappearance today in art and as a symbol of environmental movements is of the profoundest significance for humanity.

As a visual image he has three main forms. In the first and oldest form he is a male head formed out of a leaf mask; his hair, features, and physiognomy are all made either of a single leaf or of many leaves (3). In the second form he is a male head disgorging vegetation from his mouth and often from his ears and eyes; the vegetation may curl round to form his hair, beard, eyebrows and moustaches (10). The third form is a category not hitherto linked to the Green Man — for which my arguments appear later; here the head is the fruit or flower of vegetation (20). The organic combination of human head with vegetation means that, like the unicorn, the griffin and the centaur, the Green Man is a composite image. The unicorn, as a composite of a horse with the spiral tusk of the narwhal, symbolizes spiritual knowledge; it will only submit to a virgin, that is, the mind in a state of purity. The griffin, as a composite of eagle and lion, is the guardian of treasures which may include secret mysteries. The centaur, as a composite of man and horse, is the tutor of heroes, training them in courage and instinctive responses. The Green Man, as a composite of leaves and a man's head, symbolizes the union of humanity and the vegetable world. He knows and utters the secret laws of Nature. When an image of great power such as the Green Man returns as he does now in a new aspect after a long absence, the purpose of its return is not only to revive forgotten memories but to present fresh truths and emotions necessary to fulfilling the potentialities of the future.

So it is with a full eye on his present and coming significances that I have been pursuing for some years a journey of detection into the origins and past appearances of the Green Man. The investigation began in earnest for me when I was high up in one of the most beautiful towers in Europe: that of the Minster of Freiburg im Breisgau with its open fretwork spire (6 and 7). I was on the travels that led to the writing of a book on the rise of Gothic civilization.[1] Though I had long been familiar with the Green Man as an image, I was finding in the course of my travels that he was impressing himself more and more on my awareness. In the nave of the Minster below I had seen the early fourteenth-century Easter Sepulchre (21) with its life-size

6 opposite. Freiburg im Breisgau. The Minster lantern and spire completed *c.* 1340; the spire rises from the heads of the Green Men in figure 6.

14

carving of the dead Christ and the faces of Green Men looking down from the canopy above, their features contorted with grief and suffering. I had climbed the tower and reached the lantern from which you look through high pointed open arches on to the mountains and trees of the Black Forest. When you look upwards, you see the miracle of the fretwork spire with light pouring through the interstices of stone as though you were gazing at the sun pouring through the branches and leaves of a primeval tree. Following the impulse to climb as high as I could, I discovered there was a further staircase that led up above the lantern to a parapet. It is from this level that the octagon of the lantern is bent inwards, so to speak, to make the eight steep triangles of which the spire is formed. And there I had a shock: each of the ribs of the spire rose from the head of a Green Man, entirely hidden from below by the parapet (8). The progression of leaf crockets which loop up each rib, and seem to be transformed into flame forms with their ascent, rose out of the heads of these Green Men. What was this image I had thought of as pagan doing here in the supreme place of honour in this great church? I connected it immediately with the legendary forest that stretched around. I also connected it with the Green Men weeping on the Easter Sepulchre inside the Minster below. And then I thought of the significance of the number eight in medieval numerology. It is the number of rebirth and regeneration, of the complete octave and of beginning again — which is why so many fonts are octagonal. Alone up there, with the Green Men and a few jackdaws — while level with me a kestrel hovered in the distance over the town — I began to reflect on what the Green Man must have meant to the Gothic Masters. He was something I 'knew' about: I was familiar with numerous examples of him from every stage of the Romanesque and Gothic periods from the eleventh to the sixteenth centuries; after that experience I realized I hardly knew anything about him at all.

So I began to find out. The Green Man is generally treated as an amusing but often sinister survival of the old pagan religions and as a figure surviving in folk customs. My experience up the tower taught me to look at the contexts in which the Gothic Masters had carved him and as a result I discovered not only the extent to which he had been absorbed into the deepest significances of Christian art — so profoundly that it demeans the Green Man to look upon him as a mere survival of decayed beliefs — but also the universality and the ever living import of his meanings.

Clive Hicks, who took most of the photographs in this book and who was the photographer of the book on Gothic civilization, was also fired by the theme. We both discovered, whenever we gave a talk based on our earlier book, that what people most wanted to know about was the Green Man. It was as though a sleeping archetype was waking up. Artists and potters, environmentalists and ecologists, lovers of the arts and writers, deans of cathedrals and vicars of ancient parish churches, leaders of New Age thought and practising scientists had either already discovered him for themselves or were recognizing, through the writings and photographs of others as well as our own, an image that enticed them with new significances. So in addition to my questions about the Green Man in the past, I was faced with a new and imperative question: 'Why is the Green Man returning to our awareness now and what does he want from us?'

8 *Freiburg im Breisgau*. One of the eight Green Man heads from which the spire arises.

7 *opposite. Freiburg im Breisgau*. Looking up into the open work of the spire.

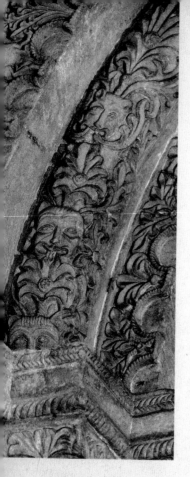

How do you speak to an archetype? Or, rather, how do you get an archetype to speak to you? One way is experiential: to let the image grow within you as you return to it time and again with the gifts of humble attention and silence. Sometimes you are given a gift in return, as I was when I was given the poem with which this book begins. As I said earlier, I only began this book after writing the poem and that drove me to the more conventional way of exploring an archetype. This is to hunt for its recurrent appearances in the past, as well as the contexts in which it appears, and to see what patterns arise.

In looking for patterns I had to remind myself that a great archetype can be revealed in many forms and that these will vary according to times and needs. We think of the Green Man as a visual image, as an object sculpted in stone or carved in wood, but the emotions he expresses transcend the form and their vitality is equally powerful when transmitted through the dance or the dramatic rituals of folk custom and in the rhythms and melodies of poetry and song. We do not only look at his leaves and blades of grass: we hear them singing and speaking to us; we touch and smell and taste his vegetation and his fruits. When an affection for a particular plant or tree is aroused in us we are linked through an emotional bond, more subtle and immediate than the effect of scent, to the greater world of vegetation of which the plant or tree is a part. It is a deep, wise world, one to which we can only respond because we possess it in our own natures and in the instinctive symbolism of the soul, in the tree of life that forms the spinal column, in the roots of our feet and legs, in the branches of our arms, and in the flowering and fruiting of our thoughts and feelings in the crown of the head.

It was the variety of his appearances that made the search for his patterns so difficult. The writings on him that explore his depths are remarkably few[2] for an image that appears in numbers probably getting into the thousands, over an area stretching from Ireland and Scotland to the cathedral of St Dimitri (9), in Vladimir, east of Moscow, built between 1193 and 1197 by Prince Vsevolod III, who employed Western sculptors.[3] It is also strange, that, given his recurrent popularity in Western art over so many hundreds of years, there are so few direct mentions of him in literature or other writings. Except for two instances (see pp.111–12), we do not know what, for example, the Gothic Masters, to whom he meant so much, actually called him.

It is only in recent years that the image as it appears in churches and other architecture has received the general appellation of the Green Man. This was owed to an article in *Folklore* by Lady Raglan published in 1939.[4] She was drawn to the image by the vicar of Llangwm Church in Monmouthshire, the Revd J. Griffiths, who showed her the examples (10) in the choir of his church hidden behind a remarkable late-fifteenth century rood screen. Griffiths thought that the image signified the spirit of inspiration but Lady Raglan decided that it represented a man and that this man was the Green Man of folklore. She also thought, after much study and travel, that the Green Man heads were portraits, taken from real life.

> ... the question is whether there was any figure in real life from which it could have been taken. The answer, I think, is that there is only one of sufficient importance, the figure variously known as the Green Man,

9 *Vladimir*. Foliate heads in the doorway of St Dimitri, 1193–7. *Alan Godfrey*.

Jack in the Green, Robin Hood, the King of May, and the Garland, who is the central figure in the May-Day celebrations throughout Northern and Central Europe.[5]

There are several assumptions in this statement shown to be unjustified by later scholarship as well as limitations of view on the scope and interest of the image. Lady Raglan also made the connexion between the Green Man and the theory of the rite of the spring sacrifice as set out by Sir James Frazer in *The Golden Bough*.[6]

Two other writers on medieval carvings in the same decade had also made a link with the Jack in the Green,[7] and it may be that a wider public had been prepared to accept Lady Raglan's name for him and her explanation of the image because of the recent success of Naomi Mitchison's *Corn King and Spring Queen*, an imaginative reconstruction of a society in the second century BC practising the rites described by Frazer with a wealth of detail and evidence. Lady Raglan's article was very influential: the name was quickly taken up and was given wider currency by its use in Sir Nikolaus Pevsner's *Buildings of England* series.

10 *Llangwm*. The Green Man on the chancel arch (fifteenth century) which inspired Lady Raglan to her researches.

19

11 *London*. 'The Green Man and French Horn': a public house sign in St Martin's Lane.

In giving the image as it appears in churches a new and evocative name Lady Raglan performed a great service. Up to her time the Green Man was known in art-historical writings by more boring and less distinctive names: in English writing, as the foliate head or even just as 'a grotesque'. In France he was called *la tête de feuilles* (the head of leaves), *le masque feuillu* (the leafy mask), or *le feuillu* (the leaf man) after the folklore figure to whom we will come later. In more recent French writings I have come across the expression *l'homme vert* but that may be a direct translation from the English. In Germany his art-historical name is the *Blattmaske*, though in German folklore there are a host of names for leaf-clothed figures in seasonal rituals including *Der grüner Mensch*.

It is undeniable that the name 'the Green Man' is ancient in origin, certainly in England and Germany. An older English name for the countryside was 'greenmans' and the great number of pubs called 'The Green Man' point both to the popularity of the name and its antiquity. There are some thirty pubs bearing that name in London alone (11) and it is particularly popular in East Anglia, where Kingsley Amis set his novel *The Green Man*. There is a twelfth-century story of a man of the woods or Wild Man who was caught by fishermen in their nets in the North Sea. He was imprisoned in Orford Castle, where he was fed on fish and could never be induced to utter a word.[8] This, however, begs the question of whether the Green Man has any connexion with the Wild Man — a matter to which we return later (p.31). There is no evidence, however, that the Green Man was ever portrayed on inn signs up to this century in his form as a head of vegetation: as a portrayal of his name he seems always to have been shown as a forester or as Robin Hood — though the signs for 'The Royal Oak' (see p.144) may well, for other reasons, owe something to his ancient and ecclesiastical connexions. When we see an inn sign today that shows the Green Man as a head of vegetation, it is almost certainly the effect of modern scholarship — and more specifically of Lady Raglan — spreading through learned brewers to popular art.

Another effect of Lady Raglan's article was, in English-speaking countries at least, for the Green Man to be seen entirely as a figure of folklore with his pagan origins emphasized. This ignores both the fact that the image was only fully developed in the context of Christian sacred art and that this development is closely linked to the rise, under the influence of Christianity, of the Western attitude to Nature which in turn gave rise to science and its industrial and technological applications.

There are, of course, in other cultures many cases of deities and spirits who are associated with plants and forests or who are portrayed coming out of foliage. There is the dangerous spirit of the Brazilian forests, Curupira, who has green teeth and green feet. His heels are in the front so that any tracker would follow him in the opposite direction from the one he travelled in. I have been told of Jain statues in which the figures have their legs clothed in leaves. I have been sent tantalizing details of an Amerindian Green Man. The Aztec corn god Xipe Tótec is the god of spring, who has to sacrifice his skin before new growth can arise. He is also the shoot of corn; in a Nahuatl poem he sings: 'Emerald is my heart. I shall see the gold water.'[9] Rich and varied examples such as these come from all over the world; but in no other culture that I am aware of has the power of the archetype been concentrated upon the human head, and this may be connected with the rise of the intellectual and objective attitude to Nature characteristic of the progress of Western thought and science. The Green Man in the form predominantly shown in this book is unknown in civilizations other than those of the Mediterranean basin and North-Western Europe, which are the chief cradles of modern science. This is a theme I will develop in the following chapters in attempting to show the Green Man as an archetypal image that reflects in his different appearances and vanishings the view held of themselves and of Nature by the people of the Western world over the centuries.

My approach to the Green Man is through several avenues of exploration, through his archetypal significances and appearances in myth and legend, through the vestiges and survivals of folk custom and ritual, through theological, philosophical, scientific and literary writings, and through the evidence of archaeology and the history of art and architecture. The two last categories will be developed in the historical treatment of the image: here I wish to say something about the archetypal significance of the Green Man and his connexions with folklore.

There are several archetypal images that are associated with the Green Man and which arise, sometimes seemingly independently of direct influences from the past, at different periods and in different places. These images include the serpent or dragon, the Great Goddess, and the sacred tree. Possibly the primal image, the one that comes closest to Jung's ultimate 'irrepresentable' archetype from which all the images derive, is that of the snake biting its tail (12).[10] It is a symbol of the relationship of eternity to time — a theme that is very important to understanding the significance of the Green Man. Because of its habit of sloughing its skin, the snake also became a symbol of rebirth. As the Ourobouros, the Great Round, the serpent devouring its tail contains within itself the created universe, the Male and Female principles, the conscious and the unconscious. From it are crystallized the images of the Great Mother and the Great Father. Within its circle appears the world island surrounded by Ocean and with the sacred tree of the universe growing in the centre of the island. From the union of the two opposites, the Sky God and the Earth Mother, is born a young god who is perpetually sacrificed, who descends to the underworld, and perpetually is reborn. This young god is the archetype of the Green Man. He is the son, the lover, and the guardian of the Great Goddess, and when she makes a new appearance in history he is bound as part of the same nexus of archetypes to reappear as well. He, like the Great Goddess, is frequently shown associated with the primal archetype of the snake. The snake also can manifest itself with wings as the dragon and we will see many instances in which the Green Man or his predecessors are shown with snakes or dragons (80 and 81). On the beautiful rood screen at Llangwm where Lady Raglan first came across the Green Man the foliage in an upper register issues from the mouth of a dragon.

The snake biting its tail has ambivalent meanings: is it devouring its own body or is it creating its body? Is it devouring time or is it creating the works of time out of its unseen essence? Which way round is the flow of time? Thus in those forms of the Green Man in which he is generally seen to be disgorging vegetation, he could also have been thought of as swallowing it. Again, the serpent biting its tail has frequently been associated with the revelation of the secrets of Nature. It appears in the earliest known alchemical

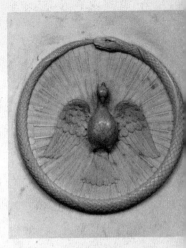

12 *Lichfield*. The snake biting its tail: the symbol of eternity on the tomb of Catherine Harper †1822 in the cathedral. The Holy Ghost appears as the Comforter in the form of a dove.

treatises from Alexandria and recurs in later alchemical and early chemical literature. It was while dozing on a bus that the chemist Kekulé in 1865 had a dream of a serpent rotating furiously as it bit its tail: this gave him the clue to the structure of the benzene ring, the discovery from which arose organic chemistry and the chemical industry with its ability to synthesize new materials which has had so profound an effect upon the world as a whole.[11]

The Great Goddess is also a symbol of matter. Mother, *mater*, matter, matrix, metre and measure all have the same root. The Great Goddess has many aspects: in some cultures she is the Earth; in others she is Sapientia, the universal knowledge that binds the cosmos together. She may be terrifying as Kali, revengeful as Ishtar or Cybele, or benign as Aphrodite, Isis and the Virgin Mary. In the Celtic and Greek traditions all her aspects are brought together as the Bride, the Matron and the Hag, as Selene-Artemis-Hecate, or as the *Deae Matres* of the Gallo-Romans. As we will see in Chapter 2, she plays a dominant part in all the myths involving the precursors of the Green Man and, if the rise of Mariolatry in the late eleventh and twelfth centuries is an instance of the Great Goddess returning in a new guise, then the return of the Green Man into sculpture at the same time shows a repetition of the pattern.

We have often been asked 'Why are there no Green Women?' There are indeed some, like those in the north aisle of the Minster of Ulm (13) or the beautiful examples at Brioude (50), but they are very rare. In Botticelli's *Primavera* the rhythm of the picture is set in motion by the blue-green god of the west wind Zephyrus flying through the branches of a tree to embrace the nymph Chloris, whose name signifies 'green'. Out of her mouth pour the flowers — just like a Green Man — through which she is transformed into the goddess Flora, the next figure in the sequence (14). From an earlier period there are magnificent vegetation goddesses to be seen in the remains of Nabataean sculpture at Petra. In general, however, the answer seems to be that, according to the nexus of myth of which the Green Man forms part, he could not exist without the feminine principle any more than mortal men can exist without mortal women. In 'Greensleeves is my delight, Greensleeves is my heart of gold' the poet sang of the Goddess, but she has many other guises in the drama to choose from, whether as the May Queen on whom the Summer Lord attends, as Isis rising from the sea, or as the Virgin either holding creation within her mantle or appearing with her Son out of foliage (16).

Another image in our nexus of archetypal images is the Sacred Tree (15). E.O. James in his wide-ranging survey of the image says, ' . . . when the secret of life was sought in nature, the Sacred Tree was the perfect symbol of its mystery, with its leaves and blossoms and fruit; either shedding its verdure in the autumn only to bring forth afresh its shoots and buds in the spring, or, if remaining evergreen, to typify life everlasting.'[12] There would seem to be few cultures in which the Sacred Tree does not figure : as an image of the cosmos, as a dwelling place of gods or spirits, as a medium of prophecy and knowledge, and as an agent of metamorphoses when the tree is transformed into human or divine form or when it bears a divine or human image as its fruit or flower. In the Vedas it is said that out of the primeval waters the gods arose 'like the branches of a tree round about a trunk'.[13] In the Bhagavad Gita the tree represents the universe;

14 Chloris, embraced by Zephyrus, becomes the goddess Flora: from Botticelli's *Primavera c.* 1478 in the Uffizi Gallery at Florence. *Mansell Collection.*

13 *Ulm.* A Green Woman on a console in the north aisle of the Minster, fifteenth century.

There is a fig tree
In ancient story,
The giant Aswattha,
The everlasting,
Rooted in heaven,
Its branches earthward:
Each of its leaves
Is a song of the Vedas,
And he who knows it
Knows all the Vedas.[14]

The cult of trees has always been of the greatest importance in Indian religion and it is often linked to the cult of sacred snakes.[15] The Yakshi or tree goddess is the indwelling spirit of the sacred tree and she is clearly linked to the cult of the mother goddess. It was under the Bodhi Tree, shining like a mountain of gold and guarded by the python, that the Buddha received enlightenment, resisting all the temptations of Mara. The Buddha was born as his mother was clasping a *sal* tree and he died on a couch set among a grove of *sal* trees.

Accounts of sacred trees are to be found in the myths of Oceania, the Americas and Africa as well as those of the Celts, Scandinavia, the Middle East, Greece and Rome, Judaism, Christianity, and Islam, which particularly contributed to the growth of Western civilization. The Koran speaks of the Lote Tree beside which the Prophet saw his second vision of the Archangel Gabriel. The Lote tree signifies the bounds of spiritual knowledge beyond which man may not pass. It has an evil counterpart in Hell — the Zaqqum tree which bears fruit like devils' heads on which sinners have to feed. Common to Judaism, Christianity and Islam is the myth of Eden with its Tree of the Knowledge of Good and Evil round which the serpent is entwined.

We will see all these archetypal images returning again and again as the story of the Green Man unfolds. An archetype can be thought of according to the older use of the term as one of the eternal ideas of Platonic and Neo-Platonic philosophy and therefore as an ever living, vital and conscious force, or in the sense in which Jung made use of it as an image from the Collective Unconscious of humanity. According to both these theories an archetype such as the Green Man represents will recur at different places and times independently of traceable lines of transmission because it is part of the permanent possession of mankind. In Jung's theory of compensation, an archetype will reappear in a new form to redress imbalances in society at a particular time when it is needed. According to this theory, therefore, the Green Man is rising up into our present awareness in order to counterbalance a lack in our attitude to Nature.

It is when one comes to the folklore theory of the origins of the Green Man that problems of transmission and of dating particularly apply. One of Lady Raglan's chief pieces of evidence for seeing him as the Green Man of folklore was an account of the ceremonies on 29 May at Castleton in Derbyshire in which a man covered in a heavy leaf-covered wicker frame rides in procession to the church. When he reaches the churchyard the leafy frame is winched off him to the top of the tower to hang there until renewed next year. The ceremony was first reported only in the last century: it may only

15 *opposite. Kilpeck.* The Tree of Life in the tympanum of the church door with the Green Man disgorging vegetation on the righthand capital, *c.* 1130.

25

date as far back as the restoration of Charles II. Also in the short time since it has been recorded there have been numerous changes in the ceremonial. She also referred to Jack in the Green: there is no evidence for this name or the context in which he appeared before the late eighteenth century (see p.149). I discovered another example of the difficulty of fitting the origins and significance of the Green Man in churches to likely connexions with folklore from consulting Van Gennep's great survey of French customs.[16] Though he found numerous examples of *le feuillu* close to the French borders of Germany — where, as we shall see, there are many examples of Green Man-like figures — he found none in a wide area surrounding Paris, the very area of the rise of Gothic architecture in the twelfth century, at which time the image of the Green Man underwent a profound transformation. This may, of course, be due to the cataclysmic effect of the French Revolution on religious and social customs in the regions closest to its centre of change: the general lack of accounts of *le feuillu* in that region, however, makes it difficult to maintain with certainty that the Green Man in his early Gothic phase was influenced by folk custom.

Much of what has been said about the connexion of the Green Man as he appears in ecclesiastical and secular buildings with folklore is presumption — a presumption based on a desire I certainly share and have to be warned against. That desire is for every tradition to be as ancient as possible. Having said that I now turn to some of the more significant accounts in which a leaf-covered figure takes part in seasonal festivities. In many of these accounts the theme of death and resurrection is clear, as in customs in Bohemia and Germany reported by Sir James Frazer such as this:

> At Niederpöring, in Lower Bavaria, the Whitsuntide representative of the tree-spirit — the *Pfingstl* as he was called — was clad from top to toe in leaves and flowers. On his head he wore a high pointed cap, the ends of which rested on his shoulders, only two holes being left in it for his eyes. The cap was covered with water-flowers and surmounted with a nosegay of peonies. The sleeves of his coat were also made of water-plants and the rest of his body was enveloped in alder and hazel leaves. On each side of him marched a boy holding up one of the *Pfingstl's* arms. These two boys carried drawn swords. They stopped at every house where they hoped to receive a present; and the people, in hiding, soused the leaf-clad boy with water. All rejoiced when he was well drenched. Finally he waded into the brook up to his middle; whereupon one of the boys pretended to cut off his head.[17]

The Musée de l'Homme at Paris contains many costumes from Czechoslovakia and Germany used in similar ceremonies, and there is an account of a ceremony performed at least until the 1950s from Thuringia in East Germany in which a leaf-covered image is carried about the village to shouts of 'The Green Man is here.'[18] At Rutten in Belgium men dressed entirely in ivy leaves sewn like dragon scales appear in the May Festivities of St Evermair.

Celebrations and ceremonies in which leaf-clad figures are key performers are not confined to spring and Whitsun. Every January the *Wilde Mann* of Basle (17), covered in leaves and brandishing an uprooted fir tree, dances in the company of a lion and a griffin to the sound of drums after sailing on a raft down the Rhine. He then leads riotous rejoicings through the streets.[19]

16 *Ely*. The archetypal Mother and Son appearing out of foliage: the Virgin and Child on a boss over the high altar in the Lady Chapel.

A better behaved but similar figure used to take part in certain church festivities in Picardy. A member of the confraternity known as the Compagnons du Loup Vert would make his way to the church of St-Firmin at Epiphany. No one dared speak to him. Wearing a green-painted wolf skin covered all over with vegetation, he would enter the church bearing a lit candle garlanded with flowers and advance at the singing of the *Gloria* to the altar, beside which he stood throughout the celebration of Mass. After the ceremony the congregation would pluck the leaves off him and bear them away with much rejoicing.[20] The ceremony was discontinued in 1727. This is one of the few examples I have come across of a Green Man taking part in a church ceremony. A still current ceremony is held on May Day at Charlton-on-Otmoor in Oxfordshire: here girls in white carry the May Cross, which is made of foliage, to the church where it is set on the rood screen. Formerly there were two May Crosses, recognizable as figures of a man and a woman.[21]

E.O. James saw the origin of the May festivities from the onwards in the Roman ceremonies known as the Magna Mater Festival (see p.38) in which Cybele 'reappeared in the guise of the May Queen and the Maypole decorated with greenery as the sacred Attis-pine'.[22] He says that as the pine tree repre-

17 *Basel*. The *Wilde Mann* on his annual journey down the Rhine in January. *Swiss National Tourist Office*.

senting Attis was taken to the Palatine temple in Rome, so in many parts of peasant Europe youths have repaired to a neighbouring wood early on May Day, after midnight, accompanied with music and the blowing of horns, for the purpose of breaking off branches of trees and adorning them with flowers. After playing games and love-making they lopped the twigs from one of the branches. Wrapping it with purple bands and decorating it with violets like the figure of Attis in Roman times, they carried it back to the village to erect it on the green or near the church. The streamers attached to the top of the Maypole and held by dancers as they plait and unplait them in their dance may descend from the bands of wool wound round the Attis-tree.

The most telling part of James's account lies in the resemblances between the reports of the Magna Mater festival and the adornment of the Maypole: otherwise most of his account of the May festivities is drawn from nineteenth-century sources apart from one hostile witness, the Puritan Philip Stubbes in the sixteenth century (see pp.133–4). We know the chief male and female characters were called the May King or Summer Lord and the May Queen, but accounts of these date only from the fifteenth century onwards and we have little idea of how the May King was dressed or adorned — though carvings at Exeter suggest splendid leafy head-dresses (18). At Thann (Haut-Rhin) there is a misericord carving showing the head of the May Queen wearing a garland next to the head of a young man wearing a cap. He is probably the Summer Lord. Both appear above the head of a Green Man.[23] There are several other heroes and characters with whom the Green Man has been linked. These include St George, Robin Hood, the Fool and the Wild Man.

St George appears in the Mummers' Plays, in which he undergoes death and resurrection. Frazer describes a rite including a simulated sacrifice among the Slavs of Carinthia on St George's Day, centred on a leaf-covered young man known as Green George.[24] Similar rites associated with St George were reported from Transylvania and from Russia. It has been recently suggested that the Mummers' Plays were brought to Western Europe in the thirteenth century by Crusaders who saw them performed in Greece.[25] This is long after the Green Man had re-emerged in art and sculpture. Others have contested the Greek source for the Mummers' Plays and it has also been suggested that the origin of our St George's story is in the Celtic sun god Belinus.[26] Did he not kill the dragon on the mound underneath the White Horse at Uffington and is not the reason why no grass grows on the summit of the mound that this is where the dragon's blood was spilt? It may be that the Mummers' Plays are a synthesis of native dramas with the story and rituals brought from Greece. What is certain is that St George was associated with the colour green: large sums were spent on dressing him in a mantle of green satin, as at Norwich in 1492. The Guild of St George, founded in 1398, was the body which arranged the St George plays, providing a dragon for the saint to fight which was a windsock banner.[27]

The legends associated with St George also stress the theme of death and resurrection. For refusing to sacrifice to Apollo he was martyred and brought to life again three times. In the first of these martyrdoms his body was dismembered and scattered over the land. St Michael brought the pieces together again and Christ restored him to life.[28] There are strong resemblances here to the legend of Osiris (p.36) and to many other vegetation myths. A Muslim writer in about AD 900 compared St George with the Mesopotamian vegetation god Tammuz (p.35).[29] Moslems also identified St George with the mysterious prophet Khidr, known as the Verdant One and whose footsteps leave a green imprint. Khidr shares his day, 23 April, with the Saint.

Plays about Robin Hood were also widely popular in the British Isles from the fifteenth century onwards.[30] The name of the famous outlaw is a contraction of Robin of the Wood. His connexion with the Green Man is strong not simply because of the green he and his merry men wore but because so many inns called 'The Green Man' portrayed him on their signs. The story of Robin Hood, who was driven to the greenwood by the wicked sheriff of Nottingham and who set up his own system of natural justice by robbing the rich to give to the poor, had a wide popular appeal. Not only did he symbolize a fairness of dealing with which people, oppressed by cruel landlords or the central authority of government, could identify; he also offered a vision of a dangerous but, at the same time, carefree life of which the sweating ploughman and the overworked apprentice could at least dream. As Robin of the Wood he also appealed to atavistic instincts, the inner certainty that the woods were wakeful and alive. He is the watcher through the leaves, the burst of laughter in an empty clearing, the joker in the ambush.

Though we can link the colour green to both St George and Robin Hood, we cannot say definitely that the portrayals of the Green Man in churches were ever consciously meant to represent either of them. If a medieval sculptor was told to carve St George, he showed him as a knight or as in his miraculous appearance in 1098 when he saved the Crusaders at the siege of Antioch by riding down the Seljuk Turks. Robin Hood was in any case not a man for stone churches.

The Green Man evades precise identifications. There is another archetypal figure, however, with whom he shares many resemblances. This is the Fool. I know of instances, the most notable being at St Wandrille in Normandy,

18 *Exeter*. A corbel carving, *c.* 1350, possibly representing the May King or Summer Lord in the cathedral nave.

where the characteristics of both images are combined. At St Wandrille he wears a foliate fool's cap and carries a cup and bauble.[31] At a deeper level the Green Man shares with the Fool the qualities of unexpectedness, of unconventional wisdom, of the joker. When we come across the Green Man, we often feel a delighted surprise as though we happened upon a child in a game of hide-and-seek and said, 'So there you are!' He helps us to find the Fool in ourselves, the uncensored response to immediate experience. At Chanteuges in the Auvergne where, as at Brioude, there are remarkable Green Men and Women in the church, every Whitsun a young man, known as *le fou* or the fool, hides in a meadow of uncut hay. He is hunted by the youths of the village and when he is caught he is dragged by the legs through the grass to be revealed to the villagers.[32]

Sometimes the Fool is linked to the Green Man in other ways. In the Scottish story (p.10) Jack is the Fool; the Green Man is the challenger and the tester of manhood. He will only take you on whether in a game or in a battle to the death if you have gold, that is, if you have something of his inner nature already. Jack could have given up after winning at cards but he insisted on going on to the final test. It is only through that test that he wins the youngest daughter. The Land of Enchantment where the Green Man lives is a strange place, free of ordinary conventions and restraints of time and space, and it is like a level of universal contact within the soul. In a variant of the story told amongst the Welsh romany gipsies of Tal-y-Llyn the hero meets the 'Green Man who lives in Noman's Land'.[33]

A figure of similar unearthly power appears in the eighth-century Irish story, *Briciu's Feast*.[34] Argument has broken out among Cuchulainn and other heroes about who is the greatest of warriors. In the course of the story a wild man or *bachlach*, hideous to look at, wearing a great bushy tree on his head 'where a winter shed for thirty calves could fit', appears in the feasting hall to offer a challenge: that a warrior can strike off his head if the wild man can do the same to him the following night. Three of the heroes on successive nights agree to the challenge, but none will submit their own necks to his axe when their turn comes. Cuchulainn alone, having struck off the wild man's head, is brave enough to take his turn. He kneels and stretches out his neck. The wild man brings his axe down with the blade turned up.

The wild man, who is the god of the other world, Cuí Ruí, in disguise, then proclaims Cuchulainn the supreme warrior of Ireland. The story is a precursor of *Sir Gawaine and the Green Knight*,[35] and Yeats was to base his play *The Green Helmet* (1910) upon it.

That kind of wild man has little to do with the Wild Men in medieval carvings. Also known as the Wodwo and the Wodehouse, the Wild Man and his Wild Woman are the aboriginal creatures of medieval lore. They are covered in shaggy hair and they live in primitive communities in forests and caves. All ancient authorities are agreed that they are deeply stupid. All modern authorities are agreed that they have nothing to do with the Green Man. I concur with this, especially on the grounds that the Green Man is supremely intelligent — but it must be said that the Green Man was and is sometimes called the Wild Man. We have the example of the *Wilde Mann* of Basle who is dressed in foliage, not in fur, to prove it. When George Gascoigne the poet appeared in front of Queen Elizabeth during her stay at Kenilworth in 1575 to recite his verses of greeting, though he was described as a Savage Man in his costume, he was in fact dressed in ivy.[36] A similar figure appeared at Cowdray (see p.10). And, given the classical and mythical associations of the Green Man and his antecedents with the sea and water, it is very possible that the Wild Man who was imprisoned in Orford Castle in the twelfth century was after all a Green Man.

If there is confusion over the names, this is not surprising given the wildness that is part of the Green Man's nature. The Wild Man is one of the animals and plants who have their abode in the demesne of the Green Man — a kingdom that contains many strange creatures such as the ghostly hunter of Windsor Forest, Herne the Hunter, or the two Green Children who were found in the Suffolk village of Woolpit in the twelfth century according to Ralph of Coggeshall.[37] The Green Man contains within himself the thrill of the hunt and of the narrow escape. London children used to play a game in which one of them was covered in grass. The others would hide and call out, 'Green Man, rise up', and the Green Man would then try to catch them.[38] When I was a boy in Cornwall, our most exciting game was a form of chain-he which we called Lincoln Green. We played it among a grove of big trees round which and through which the chain of children would wind and unwind as we chased the last stragglers.

Having made the point that the evidence for linking the Green Man as he appears in the high art of Europe over many hundreds of years with the leaf-covered figure of folk ritual is often patchy, I must state my own view which is that the archetypal force behind both the Green Man of art and the leafy figures of custom is the same. They are different manifestations of the same primal urge. They may exist concurrently, they may influence one another at certain periods, but the one is not the cause of the other because both come from a common cause — the archetype of death and renewal.

To see more deeply into that common cause we must return to the image of the sacred tree, especially in its role in rebirth, prophecy and divination. Frazer said that 'the killing of the representative of the tree spirit in spring is regarded as a means to promote and quicken the growth of vegetation. For the killing of the tree spirit is associated always ... with a revival or resurrection of him in a more youthful and vigorous form.'[39] In Christian art we will frequently find examples of the Green Man associated with the Passion and Resurrection of Christ and its linked symbolism of the wood of the Cross offering salvation 'that life should thence arise whence death had come; and that he who had overcome on the tree, should in the tree also be overcome by Christ our Lord'.[40] Whether in the mystery religions, in later folk customs or in Christianity, the resurrection of the hero or sacrificed youth was always accompanied by rejoicing and jubilation.

St Augustine says that the word jubilation derives from *jubilus*, the perpetual humming song peasants and farmers used to sing while they tended and pruned their vines and olives.[41] The leaves that issue from the Green Man's mouth are an answering song or incantation in which the spirits of trees speak to man. There are many myths and stories of trees that sing and speak. The very thought of a speaking tree implies an intelligence or spirit occupying or dwelling in the tree. The oaks of Dodona sacred to Zeus stood in a region noted for its thunderstorms: the oracle spoke through the creaking of the boughs, the rustling of the leaves and the humming of bronze gongs sus-

19 Alexander the Great with the priest of the Trees of the Sun and the Moon: from the Dutch Chapbook, *Historye van den grooten coninc Alexander.*

20 *opposite. Exeter.* The Green Man as the intelligence underlying the world of vegetation: a vaulting boss of the cathedral nave, early fourteenth century.

pended from the trees, accompanied by the cooing of doves and the purling of the sacred spring. King David would listen to the rustling of mulberry leaves in order to hear the voice of God,[42] and such stories and the many instances of the imagery of trees from both the Old and the New Testaments must have contributed to a revitalization of the symbolism of the sacred tree in the context of Christianity even as the early missionaries fought bitterly against the tree worship of ancient Europe (see Chapter 3).

One of the most popular sources of information about the ancient world in the Middle Ages was the legendary story of Alexander the Great. In the course of his conquest of the world Alexander is shown exploring the depths of the ocean and soaring high into the sky borne by griffins. In the account of his conquest of India there are variants telling of his coming across a prophesying tree or trees: in the first of these the tree has a trunk made of snakes and its fruits are the heads of women who warn him to advance no further into India.[43] In another version he travels northwards in India and enters a palace in the mountains where he is allowed to enter with few companions to meet the god of the place, who allows him to approach the Tree of the Sun and the Tree of the Moon (19). The first is all gold and the second is all silver. No sacrifices are allowed in the holy grove where they stand: Alexander kisses the bark of the Tree of the Sun and, as he is instructed, formulates his question only in his mind. The Tree of the Sun begins to answer him in the language of India and ends its message in Greek. Then he has to wait for nightfall to consult the Tree of the Moon. Again he kisses the bark of the tree and formulates his question. As moonlight falls on its silver leaves this tree begins to speak first in Greek and then in the Indian tongue. The

messages from both trees are doom-laden: he will never return home, he will die poisoned through the treachery of one of his companions, his mother will perish miserably. In the morning he is allowed to consult a naked tree on the top of which the Phoenix nests. The answers are no kinder. As he leaves, he learns that the god who allowed him to visit the trees is Bacchus or Dionysos[44] — who, as we shall see, is one of the chief precursors of the Green Man.

The stories of Alexander were probably first compiled in Egypt but acquired the trappings and spirit of chivalry as they were retold. Beyond their romantic and magical attractions, they fed the imaginations of the men of the West with an impassioned desire to know, to explore, to expand their horizons as Alexander had explored the depths and the heights and had sought out the wisest sources of knowledge, whatever the outcome or however grim the doom pronounced. In portrayals in the illuminations of manuscripts of the Tree of the Sun and the Tree of the Moon, each is shown with a gigantic head growing out of the foliage of the crown of its tree. In Prague Cathedral there are similar representations of the sun and the moon with human faces on their orbs growing out of vegetation.

The tree that speaks has a long history in Western literature: from Virgil to the Wood of the Suicides in Dante's *Inferno*, from Spenser's *Faery Queen* to Paul Valéry's poem to the Plane, from George Macdonald's *Phantastes* in which trees variously good or malign in intent guide or threaten the hero Anodos in his adventures in the course of which he dies and is reborn again, to Tolkien's *Lord of the Rings* in which the Ents or tree shepherds are among his most powerful imaginative creations. The image of the tree that speaks, prophesies or warns seems to express a recurrent need of the soul — something that we can all experience. When we stand beneath a copse of beeches roaring in a high wind, we seem to hear one of the voices of Nature only our innermost being can comprehend. It sends a messsage that indicates that nothing we claim for ourselves is ours, that the life force that sustains us is as beyond our power to control as the wind is beyond the power of the trees to resist its lashings, and that we are rooted only for a short time in history, far shorter than the lives of the beeches singing and chanting above us. When we surrender our hearts and minds to their sounds, we undergo a purification which is tinged with the feeling of sacrifice and of making holy everything we have been given — a feeling echoed by many of the finest representations of the Green Man we will come to consider.

The Green Man is the guardian and revealer of mysteries. In his mask form he is linked to the universal significances of the mask which are those of a part in a drama to be taken up and dropped again and of the world of spirits and of what lies behind death. As the disgorger or devourer of vegetation he speaks of the mysteries of creation in time, of the hidden sources of inspiration, and of the dark nothingness out of which we come and to which we return. As the fruit of vegetation, he signifies the mystery of law and intelligence in natural forms and expresses our own instinctive desire to anthropomorphize everything that is beautiful, touching or powerful in the world about us. In all his forms he is the Poet who in revealing mysteries opens up even more wonderful and enticing mysteries beyond the words he speaks.

21 *opposite. Freiburg im Breisgau.* The Green Man and the Passion: the Easter Sepulchre, 1330. Christ lies on the tomb and Green Men mourn in the canopy above.

Chapter 2

The Green Man in Antiquity

As an image concentrated on the human male head either with hair of vegetation or as a leaf mask the Green Man appears to have two main sources:
one is the mask form, which is the creation of Roman sculptors in the first
century AD; the other is in Celtic art from before the Roman conquest of
Gaul. Though these forms probably developed independently, the latter from
the Celtic cult of the human head and the former under the influence of
the mystery religions widely practised in the Roman Empire, it is likely that
both go back to a common source in prehistoric times.

   The remote origins of the Green Man are probably to be found in the religion
of Old Europe — the matriarchal religion of the Neolithic period of the first
farmers centred on and around the Danube Basin. Many of the countryside
customs (22) associated with the great festivals of the agricultural year, with
ploughing and sowing, harvesting, and the slaughter of the beasts, are considered by some to derive from these remote times in the fifth and fourth
millennia before Christ. The imagery remaining from these periods can be
related to the archetypes of the snake, the Great Goddess, the young hero
and the sacred tree. The same imagery recurs at later periods, eastwards
at Mohenjodaro and Harappa in India and westwards, as Michael Dames
has shown, at Avebury and Stonehenge.[1] In her study of the goddesses and
gods of Old Europe Marija Gimbutas has named one figure 'the ithyphallic
masked god':[2] son, lover, and guardian of the Great Goddess, he is often
portrayed in sculptures wearing a bull mask with horns. He is the god from
whom Dionysos descends and as, in turn, the Green Man first appears in
Roman art in the context of the Dionysiac mysteries, this god, although never
as far as I know in these early forms portrayed with leaves, can be seen
as an ancestor of the Green Man. Later, in ancient Greece, Dionysos was
associated both with horns and snakes and with vegetation: Euripides calls
him in *The Bacchae* 'a horned god and a god crowned with serpents'[3] and
there are accounts of rites in which a statue of simple wooden planks crowned
with branches would be raised to him. There are other accounts of his worshippers daubing their faces with red wine and wearing huge beards made of
leaves.[4] Dionysos, whether as a vegetation god, an inspirer of divine madness
and intoxication, or the revealer of mysteries of the creative force of life and
of the underworld, was one of the most universal manifestations of the archetypal common cause of the Green Man of which I spoke in the last chapter.
More will be said of Dionysos later: he, like many of the gods and goddesses
of the Middle East and the world of the Mediterranean whom we have to
consider as precursors of the Green Man, represented on all levels of understanding the sacral unity all men and women needed to feel between their

22 *Avebury*. Sarsen stones in the Kennet Avenue. It may have been a processional way for the spring festivities of the Great Goddess. Vegetation rituals still practised may go back to the time of the building of Avebury *c*. 2600 B.C.

labours in the fields, the crops that sustained their communities, their sense of belonging to those communities and the transcendental impulse to experience ecstasy and forms of awareness that took them out of the recurrent patterns of work and social life.

Thus over hundreds of years people would lament at harvest time the death of the young god Tammuz in the regions of Mesopotamia.[5] The son of Ningishzida, 'Lord of the Wood of Life', Tammuz was the beloved of Innana-Ishtar, the powerful goddess of love and voluptuousness whose cult included the practice of sacred prostitution. Similar cults were practised in Palestine, where they came into conflict with the monotheistic cult of Yahweh. These cults included those of Baal[6] and his sister-consort Anat, and also the goddess Ashtaroth or Asherah who was both a goddess of the sea and a sacred tree. Lopped trees called *asherim* sacred to her were set up in Semitic sanctuaries and they even stood in the Temple of Jerusalem — so powerful was this goddess — until the reforms of Josiah in 615 BC.

35

This goddess had her counterpart in the Lebanon in the goddess Astarte and her lover Eshmun, a vegetation god of the region of Byblos. For the Greek and Roman worlds Astarte became Aphrodite and Eshmun was known as Adonis — and their cult was to spread first to Athens and other parts of Greece and later throughout the Roman world. The chief centre of the cult was in a gorge above Byblos. In this steep, cliff-hung and water-resounding place the temple of Astarte stood until Constantine the Great had it destroyed.

In the Greek and Roman telling of the myth of Aphrodite and Adonis, Adonis is born from a tree.[7] His mother Myrrha, fleeing from the consequences of committing incest with her father, prayed when she was about to give birth to be transformed out of her human form. The prayer was answered and she was changed into a myrrh tree. The child was in the womb of the trunk and when the time came it split open to allow the birth of a beautiful boy who was to grow into an eager hunter and who attracted the love of Aphrodite. Despite her pleadings he hunted the fiercest beasts and was wounded in the groin by a wild boar, which is the beast of winter. Aphrodite came upon his mortally wounded body and in her grief she turned his blood into the red anemone flower.

Beside the temple above Byblos, at certain seasons of high water, the river turns red with particles of haematite, thus arousing the belief that it flowed with the blood of Adonis. The maidens of Byblos would weave garlands of anemone flowers in great quantities. They would fling the garlands into the river which would carry them far out to sea, so that sailors, out of sight of land, would be amazed by swathes of red water coming towards them as though the sea had turned to blood.

In Greece the chief festival was celebrated after the harvest, when women would perform the funeral rites of Adonis and would plant fast-germinating seeds in vessels which were called the gardens of Adonis. Aphrodite had laid Adonis' body on a bed of lettuce and so lettuce was included in these gardens, its quick growing and withering symbolizing the short and tragic life of the boy.

Byblos also plays a part in a profounder and even more influential legend: the story of Isis and Osiris from ancient Egypt.[8] Osiris and Isis were the children of the earth god Geb, who was sometimes represented as covered in verdure, and of the sky goddess Nut. Osiris succeeded Geb as King of Egypt and took his sister Isis as his wife. Osiris was the great civilizer and teacher: he taught his subjects the arts of agriculture, of bakery, and of making beer and wine. He built the first temples and taught men how to sculpt and to make music. Then he set out on a journey to conquer the earth by the pacific means of art and music, leaving Isis as his regent in Egypt. He travelled throughout Asia to India, subduing all peoples with his civilizing influences. When he returned to Egypt in triumph, he went to a banquet given by his brother Set, who secretly hated him and desired to rule in his stead. Set killed him by enclosing his body in a chest which was thrown into the Nile and floated out to sea. Isis, distracted with grief, went wandering in search of her husband's body. The chest had come ashore at Byblos and rested at the foot of a tree variously described as a tamarisk or a heather. The tree grew to an enormous size, enclosing the chest in its girth. The King of Byblos had the tree cut down to serve as a pillar for the roof of his palace. There it gave off so wonderful a scent that Isis heard of it and knew that it must contain Osiris' body. She travelled to Byblos where she became the nurse of the king's son. The queen Astarte came upon her one day when she was conferring the gift of immortality on the baby in her care by bathing it in flames. The startled queen interrupted her and Isis was forced to reveal her true name and her purpose in coming there. The generous king and queen gave her the trunk of the tree, from which she extracted the chest containing the body. She took the body back to Egypt, where she hid it in the swamps of Buto in fear of Set finding it. Set, relentlessly pursuing his quest of hatred, found the body, cut it into fourteen pieces and scattered them widely. Isis began her search again and regained every piece except the phallus, which had been devoured by a crab. She reconstituted his body, making a new phallus for it, and for the first time she performed on it the rites of embalmment, thereby resurrecting him to eternal life.

She subsequently conceived by Osiris their son Horus, whom she was to bring up hidden in the swamps until he could avenge his father on his uncle Set. Osiris, after his resurrection, was vindicated by a tribunal of the gods. He could have resumed the throne of Egypt but he preferred to go to the underworld, where he welcomes the souls of the good. He is represented in paintings of the underworld as having a green face (23).

The story has many meanings and levels: one interpretation of it is that Isis is the fertile plain of Egypt, flooded annually by the Nile which is Osiris. The arid desert wind which constantly tries to separate Isis and Osiris is Set. Osiris was the corn, the vine and the trees: his mummy is sometimes shown sprouting with ears of wheat. His struggle with Set is that between fecundity and aridity, between vegetation and the parched desert and between light and darkness. There were other meanings, cosmogonic, psychological and spiritual, which were taught to initiates — such as the further transformation of the green Osiris into the sun-golden Ra[9] — and it was these meanings that enabled the cult of Isis to be transported out of its native Egypt as one of the most influential of all the mystery religions of the Roman Empire, finding acceptance in the Rhineland, Gaul and Roman Britain. The appeal of the cult is movingly expressed in Apuleius' *The Golden Ass* when Lucius, who has been turned into an ass, prays to the Moon beside the sea to be restored to human form.[10] The Goddess rises from the sea, announcing herself to be the one source of all gods and goddesses, Queen Isis. With her help Lucius is changed back to human form and becomes one of her priests.

The cult of Isis lasted long after Christianity had crushed many other pagan rites and religions. Her chief temple at Philae was turned into a church only in the sixth century and many of her attributes and iconography were transferred, as we shall see, to the Virgin Mary in the Romanesque period, when the Green Man also was to appear in a new form.

The Greeks had earlier identified Isis variously with Artemis, Aphrodite, Persephone and the Eleusinian Mother of Corn at the climax of whose rites came the cry, 'The noble goddess has borne a sacred child. Brimo has borne Brimos.'[11] They also identified Osiris with Apollo, Hades, and Dionysos — with Apollo because of his civilizing influence and his cultivation of music and the arts, with Hades because of his role as lord of the underworld, and with Dionysos because of his invention of beer and wine and his association with the fertility of the earth.

23 Osiris as the Lord of the Other World giving judgment: wallpainting from the tomb of Nefertari. His face is painted green. *Werner Foreman Archive.*

24 Attis contemplates
self-emasculation while
Cupid flees in horror: 1st
century A.D. Pompei
from the house of
Pinarius Cerealis.
Alinari.

Isis was a warm, loving and tolerant goddess — unlike the terrifying goddess Cybele from Phrygia in what is now Anatolia. Crowned with the head-dress of a towered city, travelling in a chariot drawn by lions, she was dangerous to love. In her cult and legends she is associated with Attis: he was a handsome Phrygian shepherd with whom Cybele fell in love. She imposed a vow of chastity upon him which he broke when he fell in love with a water nymph. In her rage the goddess drove him to madness, in which state he castrated himself under a pine tree (24). In his remorse on coming to his senses he hanged himself on the tree. After his death he was born again and rose to be with Cybele in heaven.[12]

The centre of the cult was at Pessinus in Asia Minor, where the goddess was represented by a silver statue with the place of her features taken by a black meteoric stone. In 204 BC the Romans, at a crisis point in the Punic Wars, on the advice of the Delphic Oracle had this statue brought to Rome. The introduction of the cult was a counterbalance to the almost exclusively male Roman pantheon: it filled a need for the recognition of the power of the feminine in Roman society. What horrified the Romans, who had not made enough preliminary enquiries, was that her priests were eunuchs who had castrated themselves in her honour. They were known as *Galli* or capons. Nevertheless the Romans installed the statue in a temple on the Palatine Hill and allowed her rites to be celebrated. One of these rites was the *taurobolium* in which the devotee, to win her blessings, stood in a pit while above his head, on a perforated platform, a bull was sacrificed so that the devotee was drenched in blood. The great festival, involving public rites, took place around the spring equinox. The rites began with a procession of reed bearers on 15 March; a week later a pine tree, representing Attis, bound with clothes like a mummy and adorned with violets, was carried to the temple by tree bearers and laid to rest in the temple. This was followed by a day of mourning and then by the day of blood in which the devotees would lash themselves to draw blood, hoping to scatter it on the pine tree and so share in the passion of the god. It was then that some would perform the act of castration. The pine tree was taken to a crypt, where at dawn a young man taken to be the resurrected Attis would be found stretched out before the statue of the goddess. A day of wild rejoicing followed during which the statues of Cybele and of Attis wearing the Phrygian cap were carried to all the temples of other gods to make clear their greatness above all other deities. The resemblances of these rites to the story and ritual of Easter have often been commented upon: the comparison has been made between the entry of the reed bearers to Palm Sunday and the carrying of the tree to Christ's carrying of the cross; and there are strong similarities in the mourning of the death and the resurrection from the tomb, as well as, of course, in the time of the ceremonies.[13] As was noted earlier, comparisons have also been made between the later spring and May festivals of Europe which may descend in part from the rites of Cybele (see p.27). The cult was certainly spread widely throughout the Roman Empire, and if I mention it here at some length it is because of the resemblances between Attis and the Green Man, first in the sacred tree bearing the image of the god, second in the possible effect of the rites of Cybele on later folk customs, and third in the resurrection theme as will be seen in the frequent association of the Green Man with this theme in the context of Christian iconography.

There is much less conjecture in the association of Dionysos with the Green Man. Dionysos was called, among a host of epithets that reflect the immensity of his nature, the 'twice mothered' (Dimetor) and the 'thrice born' (Trigonos). These names come from a sequence of legends that begin with the union of Zeus with Persephone.[14] Dionysos under the name of Zagreus was the fruit of this union and Zeus intended him to be his heir. Jealous Titans killed the child, cutting up and devouring all his body except his heart, which was saved by Athene. Zeus took his vengeance on the Titans by reducing them to ashes, from which the race of mankind arose. From the heart of Dionysos a love potion was made: this was given to Semele, daughter of the King of Thebes, so that she should fall in love with Zeus. Dionysos was reborn in her womb. Prompted by the jealous Hera, Semele demanded to see Zeus in his divine form. The revelation of the god was so powerful that Semele was consumed, though the child was rescued from her remains. Zeus sewed the foetus up in his thigh until it achieved its full term and was born once more as Dionysos. He was brought up on honey by nymphs knows as the Hyades and was attended in his youth in Thrace by satyrs and sileni. He discovered wine and, after rescuing his mother Semele from Hades, he set off on a journey to India, introducing the world to the delights of wine, ecstasy and intoxication. Like Osiris he taught knowledge of agriculture and the arts though, as the story of *The Bacchae* shows, his appearance in a community could have devastating effects on any who resisted his powers. In the course of his adventures he set sail in a ship whose sailors tried to kidnap him for a great ransom. Dionysos made a vine grow out of the deck and ivy to twine about the rigging. The oars turned into serpents and he himself became a lion while the ship was filled with beasts and with the sound of flutes, so frightening all the sailors that, except the helmsman who had stood by the god, they jumped overboard where they turned into dolphins.[15]

From the cult of Dionysos sprang the widely practised rites of the Bacchantes and maenads, the women who sought union with him in frenzied ecstasy. From the satyr plays rose the great tradition of Greek drama; the statue of Dionysos always stood in a place of honour on the stage. There also arose one of the most popular mystery religions of the Roman Empire, centred on his myths. This mystery religion would seem to have encompassed every range of religious behaviour, from rites in which the Bacchantes ate raw flesh in imitation of the Titans devouring Zagreus and as a kind of communion with the god, to the most sublime Neo-Platonist interpretation of the myths. This interpretation is particularly interesting both for itself and for its implications for how the Gothic masters may have seen the Green Man at a later date. According to this view Dionysos is identified with the Mind of this world, the 'mundane intellect'. Dionysos, according to Joscelyn Godwin, is a creative deity as the child of the cosmic creator, Zeus. From Dionysos comes the idea of the world which is sustained in its reality by his knowledge. Through his dismembering by the Titans he enters into the human race and is the higher mind in all of us.[15]

The same author says that the thyrsus, the wand carried by the Bacchantes, made from a fennel stalk topped by a pine cone, symbolizes the spinal column culminating in the pineal gland through which is reflected this higher faculty of knowledge and inspiration.

25 Maenads dancing in front of a leaf clad statue of Dionysos: a drawing after a *stamnos* by the Dinos painter *c.* 420 B.C., Naples. *Mansell Collection.*

26 *Pfalzfeld*. The St Goar pillar showing the leaf head of a deity, *c.* fifth century B.C. *After Anne Ross*, Pagan Celtic Britain, *1967.*

There were many representations of the god. One used in initiation rites was a huge bearded mask wreathed with vine or ivy leaves (25). This was laid on a winnowing basket to conceal the sacred symbols, including a phallus made of figwood. Sometimes Dionysos is shown as an old man at the point when he goes to the underworld and he is also mysteriously in this underworld aspect identified with Okeanos, called by Homer the origin of the gods.

The appeal of the mystery religions in the Roman Empire was owed not solely to their dramatic and ecstasy-arousing rites but because they filled a great lack in the Roman state religion. This lack was the absence of any developed conception of an afterlife. In contrast the mystery religions could provide experiences that offered a foretaste of future bliss and assurance for the bereaved that those they had lost survived in a fuller existence. Thus the great historian Plutarch wrote to his wife on the death of their daughter begging her to console herself with the assurance of immortality to be found in traditional belief and in the Dionysiac mysteries.[16]

The Celtic races, according to Caesar, had a firm belief in the immortaility of the soul, and it is to their religion and art that we go northwards to find another god who was probably as important as Dionysos in his contribution to the development of the image of the Green Man.

This is the Celtic god Cernunnos.[17] He too is probably a descendant of the same lover of the Goddess from whom the ancestry of Dionysos is traced. Dionysos, from being a god of beer, turned into the god of wine and his sway, until the Roman conquest of North-West Europe, was limited to the wine-growing regions of the Mediterranean. His distant cousin, however, was a god of the forests. Often portrayed with antlers growing from his brow, he was attended by deer and snakes and other wild animals, and he too suffered death and exile in the underworld. He is also shown sometimes with hair of vegetation. Most representations of him are of the period after the Roman conquest and settlement of Gaul and Britain, but there are two outstanding works of art that predate the conquest and that reveal many of the Celtic elements that were to be fused in later representations of the Green Man.

The first is a carving known as the St Goar pillar from the Hunsrück in West Germany (26).[18] Described as a phalloid cult figure, it was originally six foot high. It is carved with a head with vegetation on the brows and forming the beard, which represents Cernunnos. The decoration seems to blend an Etruscan influence with the native style of the La Tène culture of the Celts, and the pillar is thought possibly to date to the fifth century BC. Here there is a clear connexion between fertility and the leaf head, as well as an early indication of the cult of the human head which was such a feature of Celtic religion and art.

The second and far more famous object is the Gundestrup Cauldron (27 and 28), now in the National Museum in Copenhagen. It is a huge embossed silver-gilt bowl formed of hammered plates of silver, with staring heads around the exterior and with scenes of gods and animals on the inside. The centre plate of the base contains the raised figure of a bull, virile, proud and fierce. Though illustrations of it may be familiar to my readers as they were to me before I went to see it, none of these convey the impact of being in the presence of the cauldron itself. It is numinous with life, glittering with memories and emotions cast off from its beaten and chased plates. It is as

27 Cernunnos as a horned deity surrounded by animals on an inner plaque of the Gundestrup Cauldron, First century B.C. *Nationalmuseet, Copenhagen.*

28 The head of Cernunnos with his hair formed of leaves and his arms holding up two deer; on an outer plaque of the Gundestrup Cauldron. *Nationalmuseet, Copenhagen.*

though you have come into the presence of one of the legendary cauldrons of Celtic mythology — Cerridwen's pot or the inexhaustible cauldron of the Dagda.

Its placing in its present home, which is one of the most splendid museums in Europe, creates all the more dramatic an impression because you come to it guided through a progression of galleries rich with the artefacts and tombs and bodies of even earlier generations; piled hoards of dark orange amber, the trade in which extended from the Baltic to the Peloponnese; the dresses and ornaments of a Bronze Age princess; the glorious Sun Chariot of Trundholm with its disk overlaid with gold beaten in labyrinthine patterns; and the remains of those who in the very period of the cauldron itself were sacrificed and — like the cauldron itself — given to the waters of a bog.

That is where it was found in 1891 — in a bog at Gundestrup.[19] The cauldron was probably made in Gaul in the first century BC. No one knows why or how it reached Denmark, though it was perhaps a gift to some important Northern princeling.

Much of what is finest in Celtic art has been recovered from bogs, pools, rivers and streams. The Celts venerated water and they would throw into water or bury in bogs not only the crania of their dead and the corpses of chosen sacrificial victims but also weapons and works of art of the highest standards of workmanship. From many cultures we are familiar with the practice of human and animal sacrifice; we are also familiar with the practice of furnishing tombs with rich artefacts: what is totally unfamiliar to us is the deliberate offering up and willing loss of superb works of art. The possession of such treasures must have added greatly to the prestige of a ruler and therefore to the tribes or clans over which they ruled. They would have been sacrificed therefore only at times of special need, and perhaps the need itself dictated what particular kind of artefact should be sacrificed. Just as into the healing waters of the Goddess Sequana at the source of the Seine were thrown sculptures of the afflicted parts of the bodies of those seeking cures, so the Celts may have sacrificed the appropriate symbol of what they particularly needed. Thus, the Gundestrup Cauldron — the symbol of fruitfulness and plenty — may have been allowed to sink into the bog at a time of great dearth.

The sacrifice of works of art would have been no slight on the smiths and craftsmen, who were honoured in their hierarchies as were druids and bards. These artists could take base and precious metals and work them into marvellous and beautiful shapes instinct with life and meaning: they could imbue matter with spiritual and sacramental purpose through their flowing triskele patterns and their bold staring faces so that, on behalf of their people, the gods could be honoured and propitiated. Sometimes, it is thought, they made artefacts deliberately for the purpose of sacrifice — that they should be thrown into water never to be seen again except by the gods to whom they were given. It is as though they gave back gifts to the source of creativity in return for those they had received, confident that, because they did not cling on to their works, the inspiration would return for the creation of new beauty.

The fate of the Gundestrup Cauldron seems to proclaim a message from the Celts: just as the vegetation of the earth must die for it to be renewed again, so the beauty of art must be destroyed or hidden for new art to arise — a message implicit in the myths and images that were to be fused into the Green Man.

Death, metamorphosis and rebirth are themes in the Celtic myth that has been deduced from the Gundestrup Cauldron and from later Gallo-Roman works of art by Jean-Jacques Hatt.[20] He says that at the centre of this myth is the mother goddess who marries first a sky god, Taranis, and then an earth god, Esus-Cernunnos. This earth god is known as Esus in the spring when he is the god of vegetation and the lover of the Great Goddess, and after his death as Cernunnos who is half man and half stag. Cernunnos becomes the god of the underworld, like Osiris, and of riches, like Pluto. Esus-Cernunnos returns to become the lover of the Goddess again at the end of winter through the help of a human hero called Smertrius who bears many resemblances to Hercules. Smertrius kills one of Taranis' watchdogs; in revenge for this and for being deserted by the Great Goddess, Taranis turns the Great Goddess and her two attendants into cranes. Smertrius restores them to human form by sacrificing three divine bulls and then he sacrifices a stag to enable Cernunnos to return to earth and marry the Goddess.

All these incidents in the story can be traced in the Gundestrup Cauldron, including the turning of the Goddess into a crane and the magnificent bull in the bottom of the cauldron with its head raised as Smertrius with drawn sword approaches it. It is, however, with Cernunnos as portrayed here that we are particularly concerned. He is shown both as a complete figure on an interior plaque and as a head on the exterior.

In the interior plaque he appears in a position that recalls a yogic asana (27). There is a similar portrayal of an antlered god on a seal from Harrappa two thousand years earlier in date. This is said to represent the god Pasupati, who is an aspect of Shiva.[21] In his left hand Cernunnos holds a serpent, which is sacred to the goddess, and in his right a torque neckband with which he will marry the Goddess. A deer and wolf approach him respectfully. Antlers grow from his head and from one of these sprouts a stylized tendril of leaves.

The representation of Esus-Cernunnos on the exterior of the cauldron shows him much closer to the form of the Green Man or foliate head (28). First, his hair is portrayed as stylized vegetation and, second, the power of the image is concentrated on the head, though here his arms are also shown holding deer by the hind legs.

This concentration on the head is particularly important to the development of the Green Man for the following reasons. The human head, either severed or considered on its own, was an object of particular veneration to the Celts. It was the seat of inspiration, foreknowledge, prophecy; it promoted fertility and could act as a guardian to drive away evil forces.[22] They placed skulls in their shrines, as at Roquepertuse. They would put them round their buildings and over their gateways. They also carved the human head in wood and stone and would set the carvings in auspicious places. Many heads of Cernunnos have been found with holes for inserting antlers or vegetation. Some heads have two or three faces. The practice of placing roughly carved heads in stone walls of fields to promote fertility certainly continued into the present century in Britain[23] and may still be a current rite. The veneration of the head survives in many legends — of heads that spoke by sacred wells, of Bran the Blessed whose head continued to be a delightful companion after he was decapitated. His head was placed on the site of the Tower of London to guard the country from invasion.[24]

As Rome extended her boundaries over more and more regions, including those of the Celts, so, as we have seen in the cases of Isis and Cybele, there was a reverse process whereby the cults of the people she conquered were established in the city of Rome herself. New artistic styles could well arise from the syncretism of religions brought about in a common centre of civilization. It would be tempting to see the influence of the Celtic cult of the head in the first appearance of the foliate mask or Green Man in Roman art of the first century AD, but there is no evidence for this. Though Cernunnos appears frequently in the remains of Gallo- and Britanno-Roman art, in some cases absorbed into the Roman pantheon — as in the case of a funeral monument at Rheims where he is flanked by Apollo and Mercury — he does not appear to have entered imperial art at this period. The fusion of the two strands probably took place later, perhaps, curiously enough, under the influence of Christianity.

What links all the legendary stories, whether from Northern Europe or the Middle East, is the theme of metamorphosis. Metamorphosis is also a constant theme in Greek and Roman mythology. If Dionysos had a varied career in animal forms, he had inherited the tendency from his father Zeus, who was capable of infinite invention for the shapes in which he conducted his love life. Nearly all the Immortals had the same capacity, whether for their amours or their power struggles and intrigues. Their deeds and transformations are fully described in Ovid's great poem, *Metamorphoses*. One of Ovid's most charming episodes is that of another god, Vertumnus the god of autumn fruits, who fell in love with the beautiful and disdainful goddess of orchards Pomona, who rejected all her suitors. Vertumnus changed from a haymaker to a harvester and other forms — all without success until he turned into an old woman who told Pomona about a handsome young god called Vertumnus and awakened her interest. Then, suddenly, he turned into his own true form, ardently pressed his suit and won her love.[25]

The theme of metamorphosis entered Imperial Roman art in the period of Augustus and during Ovid's lifetime. It was not always approved of. Vitruvius writes of the 'improper taste of the present' in which, instead of columns, there rise up stalks; instead of gables there are panels with curled leaves and volutes. 'Candelabra uphold pictorial shrines' and above these 'clusters of thin stalks rise from their roots in tendrils with little figures seated on them at random'. He speaks here also of stalks ending in the half bodies of men and of animals.[26] Perhaps the most influential paintings in the style are in Nero's Golden House on the Palatine Hill in Rome. The paintings there are the origin of the grotesque figures of the Renaissance period. The excavated rooms of the Golden House were known as caves or *grotte*, and the word grotesque for the composite figures formed from humans, birds and beasts derives from this. One of the features of architecture during the reign of Augustus had been the splendid sculptures of vegetation, as may be seen in the Ara Pacis in Rome, or in the exquisitely carved fruits and flowers in the arch at Glanum, near St-Rémy, where they signify the fruits of civilization the Roman conquest had brought to the Gauls. The delight in accurate observation of leaf and fruit forms was a necessary precursor to the appearance of the foliate head. The accuracy that had been achieved in Roman portrait sculpture was applied to the vegetable world and the instinc-

29 Two capitals showing female deities rising out of acanthus leaves, 2nd century A.D. in the Cirencester Museum. *After Anne Ross,* Pagan Celtic Britain, *1967.*

tive human need to anthropomorphize natural forms — which is akin to meta-morphosis — took over through the new element of playfulness that can be seen in the grotesques of the Golden House. People and animals appear in what are called peopled or inhabited scrolls.[27] Men, women and children were depicted as half figures: that is, human figures naked to the waist arising out of curlicues of leaves.

In addition to their associations with particular gods and legends, certain of the plants portrayed had significances of their own which helped to decide how and where they should be used. One example of this is the acanthus leaf and its use in the Corinthian column. Vitruvius says that Callimachus, the architect who devised the Corinthian column, was visiting Corinth to fulfil a commission.[28] He came upon the tomb of a young girl whose mourning nurse had placed on it a basket containing the cups her charge had delighted to use when she was alive. To protect the cups she had placed a big tile on top of the basket. An acanthus plant seeded itself in the stone of the tomb and one of its fronds, its growth checked by the tile, had curled over in a natural volute. This gave Callimachus the inspiration for introducing a new order into architecture — and one that because of this story associated the acanthus with death and rebirth. An adaptation of the Corinthian capital, popular in a wide area from North Africa to Germany, was the Jupiter column, in the capital of which the heads of the god and other deities were carved surrounded by acanthus fronds.[29] This theme, like the peopled scrolls and half figures, seems to arise from a desire to anthropomorphize vegetation — to draw out the hidden intelligence in plant forms and to give them human forms and faces, a current that was to arise again in Romanesque times (29).

30 Okeanus as the transformation of Bacchus with his beard made of seaweed: a detail of the Okeanus dish from the Mildenhall Hoard, *c.* A.D. 200, British Museum. *Bridgeman Art Library.*

The chief origin for the Green Man in Roman Imperial art would seem to be the mystery religions, particularly the Dionysiac rites. As the Green Man first appears as a leaf mask, the most obvious source for this would seem to be either the mask of Dionysos used in initiation ceremonies, or theatrical masks. In many of his representations he is shown as a sad elderly face and may thus be representing the ageing Dionysos who descends to the underworld and becomes identified with the universal image of Okeanos. He is to be seen in this form in a frieze on the Temple of Bacchus at Baalbek (*c.*AD 150). He also appears on the two triumphal arches erected in Rome by Septimius Severus who, with his wife Julia Domna, a Syrian priestess, was a keen supporter of the mystery religions. Later he is assimilated to the solar cult of Aurelian and appears in that Emperor's Temple of the Sun (*c.*AD 270). He is also to be seen in a temple at Hatra in Mesopotamia with snakes writhing in his hair, a representation that has been compared to the famous male Medusa head at Bath. Some of the best evidence for seeing him as arising from the cult of Dionysos is in tomb sculpture carved with leaf masks which may represent the point at which the dying are transformed into the universal world of Dionysos-Okeanos. This theme appears also in the Okeanos dish from the Mildenhall hoard in the British Museum: at the centre of this splendid silver platter surrounded by rejoicing maenads and satyrs, the head of Okeanos stares out with dolphins in his locks and a beard of seaweed sprouting from his chin (30).

The association of the image with death and rebirth was clearly established at an early stage in its history. It is on a tomb that the Green Man is first

31 *Poitiers*. The earliest known example of the Green Man as the disgorger of vegetation on the tomb of St Abre, in St Hilaire-le-Grand, *c.* A.D. 400.

to be seen in a Christian context. This is on the tomb of St Abre, daughter of the apostle of the Gauls, St Hilary, now preserved in St-Hilaire-le-Grand at Poitiers (31). The tomb is thought to be of the fourth or fifth centuries. He is carved on the side of the lid of the sarcophagus, and he also seems to develop a new theme in the history of the Green Man. Not only is his head rayed with vegetation but scrolls of leafy branches issue as his moustaches or from his nostrils (the carving is worn and it is hard to make out their exact source). This may represent a transitional stage in the process through which the Green Man becomes the disgorger of vegetation.

Clever Green Man! Innumerable other images die or go to sleep under the impact of Christianity. He, together with the sacred tree and the imagery of the vine, survives because of his irrepressible vitality. The sacred tree was absorbed at an early stage by the Christians.[30] By the third century the Tree of Life was described as the centre of the world at Golgotha with a holy spring at its feet from which all nations would drink and rise to salvation through its branches. In *The Shepherd of Hermas* a lopped willow is described as a cosmic tree overspreading the earth, symbolizing the Son of God. The twigs of the willow are the Law of God.[31] To many of the early Christians, Christ was the fulfilment and the revealed truth behind the mystery religions that the new religion would supplant. He had said, 'I am the true vine', and as the vine He was allegorized as the bringer of eternal life to the faithful on both sides of the grave. The resurrection imagery of the Dionysiac rites was thus a lawful seizure by conquest of the new religion. The imagery of

the vine is to be found throughout Christian art, especially in Byzantium and its areas of influence. It was, perhaps, through this adoption of the symbolism of Dionysos that the Green Man was absorbed into Christian art. Thus from Mudanya on the Sea of Marmara there comes a magnificent series of capitals of the sixth century, showing huge Okeanos faces formed of acanthus leaves and with vibrant and staring expressions (32). Similar capitals of the same period have been found in Istanbul,[32] though the image seems to have had no later history in Byzantine art after the time of the Iconoclasts.

There is one region above all to which we have to go to see the meeting point of the southern and the northern strands that went into the Green Man and also into Christianity. This is in and around Trier, the most ancient city of Germany, founded by the Romans beside the Mosel in AD 14. Long before the Romans the valley of the Mosel was inhabited by the Celtic tribe of the Treveri, part of the Hunsrück-Eifel culture which produced the St Goar pillar (26). The Romans introduced the cultivation of the vine to the Mosel and the reputation of the region for the quality of its wines dates from this period. The Landesmuseum in Trier contains a series of tombs of the wine merchants and their families.[33] Some of these tombs were huge in size and even their fragmented remains are impressive. They are in fragments because in the later Roman Empire the cemetery was used as a quarry for a fort built at Neumagen to resist invaders. Walking among these sepulchres and sculptures, I felt I had rarely come across tombs which expressed so cheerful and practical a certainty in the life to come. The world of immortality for those

32 Okeanus heads on a capital from Mudanya, 6th century, now in the Archaeological Museum, Istanbul. *Kathleen Basford.*

47

33 A foliate head from
the Schulreliefpfeiler
from Neumagen, c. A.D.
200, Landesmuseum,
Trier. *Kathleen Basford*.

who have made good wine and practised the mysteries of Bacchus is a glorious
and permanent promise of enjoyments that in life have been fleeting. The
souls of the dead, guided by a happy steersman, travel off to their destination
in boats laden with wine barrels, amphorae and baskets of fruit. On many
of the tombs foliate heads (33), serious and watchful, full of the tiredness
of harvest, await transformation — they are the aged Dionysos about to go
to the other life. In the pediments we see what the god will be transformed
into: the leaf-rayed, open-eyed god Okeanos, surrounded by dolphins, who
is the goal of the souls in the boat and into whom they will be merged to
become part of his universal immortality.

Trier became a favourite city of several Emperors including Constantine
the Great, and under them the present cathedral was built. The city became
a centre of the spread of Christianity. Then came the invasions of the barbar-
ians: the city was seized four times in the fifth century, the last time by
the Franks who burned the cathedral. Bishop Nicetius (AD 526-566) rebuilt
the cathedral and in order to get stone he plundered the remains of a nearby
temple of the Hadrianic period at Am Herrenbrünnchen. In doing so he carried
out an act of the greatest significance for the full adoption of the Green Man
into Christian art.[34] He took giant composite capitals each carved on four
sides with leaf masks and set them up on piers round the crossing of his
reconstructed cathedral (34). The leaf masks were painted yellow and red.
The crossing may have been particularly important for the display of relics,
of which Trier possesses many notable examples, among them the seamless
robe of Christ and one of the nails from the Crucifixion. These leaf masks,
set in a place of honour in one of the most important churches in Christendom,
therefore could impress themselves on the minds of the clergy, merchants

34 A cast of one of the now concealed foliate heads, originally from the 2nd century Am Herrenbrünnchen Temple and placed in Trier Cathedral by Bishop Nicetius, Landesmuseum, Trier. *Kathleen Basford.*

and other travellers as an image that should by right be present in a church. They exerted this influence for some five hundred years until in the course of the eleventh and twelfth centuries they were walled up when the crossing was rebuilt.[35] They were rediscovered in the last century and re-examined in 1961-2. A window has cleverly been cut in the north-west pier of the crossing so that you can now see the great grim face of one of these notable Green Men. Even if these were hidden, the Green Man was to flourish and to multiply many times in the Romanesque and Gothic sculpture of the city as well as in the architecture of later periods.

What was Bishop Nicetius up to in placing these Green Man heads from a pagan temple in such prominent positions? Was he simply making use of fine capitals and not worrying about the significance of the figure sculpture? Or did he see in them, as perhaps had the patrons who commissioned the image on the tomb of St Abre, a symbol of rebirth and immortality so universal that it could transcend any worries about their pagan provenance? Or was he asserting the power of Christ over the elemental forces that inspired the tree worship of the pagan populations he and his fellow clerics and missionaries had the duty to convert?

Chapter 3

The Green Man in the Dark Ages

A woman is taking an axe to a tree. From the crown of the tree two heads rise up aghast at what she is doing. They are the spirits of the sacred tree. A bishop stands to one side blessing her action; there are other people marvelling as they look on. This scene is shown in a twelfth-century manuscript[1] of the life of St Amand who, five centuries earlier, had brought about the destruction of sacred groves of oaks. According to the story the woman was a pagan and she was also was blind; when St Amand converted her, he put an axe into her hand and told her to cut down the tree. When she had done so, her sight was restored to her.

The story is a parable of a process that has been called the greatest psychic revolution in the history of our culture.[2] This was the victory of Christianity over paganism, in particular over the cults of the tree and the sacred spring. The revolution was, I believe, to have a profound effect on the later development of the Green Man. The woman who has her sight restored by chopping down the sacred tree is an emblem of humanity beginning to see and interpret Nature in a new way. If the Green Man signifies the relationship of man to Nature, then the way in which he is portrayed will change with changes in that relationship. He does indeed change during the Dark Ages, because it was in this period that he took on fully his new form as the disgorger and devourer of vegetation.

The Dark Ages have been described as a period in which, because of the breakup of Roman rule, it was possible for technological innovations to be introduced without the resistance they would have received in a more ordered state of society. Among these were the heavy plough, the stirrup and the more general adoption of the watermill.[3] The heavy plough was to lead to the exploitation of the heavy alluvial soils of North-West Europe on a scale unknown to the Romans during their long period of colonization. The opening up of the potential wealth of those regions was to create eventually the surplus that built the cathedrals, restored city life and won the Holy Land. Its introduction also brought about new organizations of villages grouped round a church and a manor. In addition, its use signified a new attitude on the part of humanity to their mother Earth: they were prepared to wound her more deeply than ever before for their own subsistence and gain. Lynn White, on remarking that nowhere else in the world did farmers develop an agricultural implement analogous to the heavy plough, asks, 'Is it coincidence that modern technology, with its ruthlessness towards nature, has so largely been produced by descendants of those peasants of Northern Europe?'[4]

This attitude is part of a more general effect which the same historian attributes to the influence of Christianity. By the eighth century Christian missionaries had been successful in winning men to a certain extent from the animism of the past. The worship that had been given to the gods and goddesses of Nature was transferred to the shrines and relics of the saints. Embargoes on clearing forests once considered sacred, or diverting waters that were holy, no longer possessed their old authority. Lynn White sees the changes markedly in the portrayals of the Labours of the Months in Carolingian manuscripts. Though these follow a tradition laid down in classical times, what is different between them and their antique models is that the older models show the months as passive symbols while the new ones show men delving the earth and hacking and hewing at Nature.[5] Man was becoming ready to assert his mastery over Nature and the spirits of Nature with a new and frightening energy.

In a later representation of the Labours of the Months in the carvings round one of the west front doors of the Abbey of St-Denis (*c.*1130) we find the Labours, contained within vegetation scrolls that issue from the heads of Green Men, separating each month from another. The vigorous activities of the figures exactly portray this new attitude just as the presence of the foliate heads indicate a new aspect of the Green Man: as the source and goal of the products of time.

The examples of the Green Man at Trier Cathedral and the tomb of St Abre at Poitiers (31) demonstrate that the image had been absorbed into Christian iconography in the late Empire and by the time of the beginning of the Dark Ages. The world from which he came, however, the world of forests and holy groves, of sacred rivers and pools, still resisted Christianity. Emile Mâle says that everything we now see as beauty was for the Celts religion: 'The forest was divine.'[6] The energies Christians could spare from their internecine quarrels and accusations of heresy had frequently to be devoted to destroying the hold that tree worship still maintained over the lives and imaginations of men and women. Though examples of the Green Man image in sculptural remains are comparatively few in the period from the sixth to the beginning of the eleventh century, it was in those centuries that the long, slow transformation in the attitude of Western humanity to Nature took place which was essential to the way in which, during the Middle Ages, the Green Man made a bridge from his pagan origins to a fresh life in the context of Christian art.

This was brought about by the relentless attacks of saints and missionaries on those beliefs and practices of the pagan past they could not incorporate into Christian ritual. Thus in the fifth century St Martin of Tours ordered that a much revered pine tree should be cut down: the woodcutters agreed to do it only on condition that he stood directly in the path of its fall. He did so without hesitation and, at the moment when it was about to fall on him, he made the sign of the cross. The tree raised itself up again and fell on the opposite side.[7] The feelings of those who held to the old ways and lamented the coming of this new religion that practised such sacrilege in the name of a higher love are recorded, for example, in the legends of St Patrick's conversations with ancient heroes such as Oisin who returns to earth to mourn the changes he finds. We know, also, of the strength and continuity of these feelings from the frequent denunciations by churchmen and Christian monarchs of pagan practices and of the many cases in which these survived into modern times. Thus Emile Mâle describes seeing in the

35 *Calne*. Avenues of yew trees in the churchyard which occupies a prehistoric site.

region of Bagnoles-de-l'Orne trees hung with stones which had been placed there by sick people. Each stone represented a particular illness which the tree would cure.[8]

In many cases the Church took over rites from the past and blessed them. The ceremony of well-dressing in Derbyshire probably descends from the Celtic love of holy springs. The presence of yews in so many churchyards is not just a reminder of death and of the evergreen nature of the soul: it is an example of how a tree venerated in the old religion was planted with a new symbolic meaning given it so that the psychic power associated with it could be transferred to the new religion. The church and churchyard with its many yews at Calne (35) in Wiltshire stand on what is thought to be the site of a prehistoric henge monument. Another churchyard most celebrated for its yew trees is that of Painswick, a hilltop town in Gloucestershire. There are so many yew trees there clipped into ancient avenues that it as though you enter a living henge when you visit it. Trimming the yews at Painswick on 19 September is followed on the next Sunday by the ceremony of the Church Clipping in which the parishioners form a ring round the church and kick it to show their affection for it. These yearly customs are thought to be an example of the Church giving its blessing to an old.[9]

One of the most dramatic stories of this period in this connexion concerns the eighth-century Anglo-Saxon missionary to Germany, St Boniface. The turning point in his mission came when he summoned the people of Hesse, who were deeply attached to tree worship, to meet him at the sacred oak of Thor at Geismar. In their presence he struck at the oak with an axe, and a gust of wind broke off the topmost branches. He continued to cut away at the tree until its trunk burst into four parts of equal length, lying in the shape of a cross. He then had the wood used to construct a chapel dedicated to St Peter. His chronicler Willibald said that the heathen who had come to curse returned home to bless and praise Christ.[10] St Boniface was later to be martyred by pagans in Frisia in 755; he had by that time, however, made mighty inroads upon the old beliefs.

An interpretation of recent research may throw light on why he was so ferocious in his work of destruction and why he was so determined to win the power of the trees to Christ. He came from Crediton in Devon, not far from the village of Bow where recently the remains of a Bronze Age wood-henge or tree temple have been discovered. Many of the local villages bear the words Nymet, Nymph or Nympton in their names: all derive from the Celtic word *nemeton*, meaning a sacred place or sacred grove. The two churches nearest the henge, Broadnymet and Nymet Tracy, were both originally dedi-cated to St Martin of Tours who, as we have seen, was a fearless opponent of tree worship. It seems likely therefore that Boniface was brought up in a region where tree worship was particularly strong and that he had deep personal knowledge of the forces against which he had to fight and then to win for Christ.[11] In his part of Devon the churches possess an exceptional number of Green Man carvings of the fourteenth and fifteenth centuries such as those at Sampford Courtenay (36), South Molton (109) and King's Nympton (5), and it has been suggested that this is because of a continuing attachment to the religion of the trees. (But see p. 122.)

It must be remembered that the old gods and spirits of Nature were not to the masterful saints of the Dark Ages illusions or superstitious fantasies as they are to the sophisticated modern mind. They were genuine demonic forces who could appear to them at times and frequently tormented and worsted them. The need for protection against these forces appears in St Patrick's hymn known as 'The Deer's Cry', which he made one day when his enemies, the druids at Tara, were about to attack him and his servant. As he uttered the hymn his enemies could only see a wild deer and a fawn. The hymn includes this passage where he calls on the strengths of God's power, wisdom, eye, ear, word, hand, shield and host 'against incantations of false prophets; against black laws of heathens; against false laws of heretics; against craft of idolatry; against spells of women and smiths and druids; against every knowledge forbidden to the souls of men'.[12]

When St Paul spoke of the powers, dominations and elemental forces that had ruled the world until the coming of Christ,[13] he did not say that they were fantasies: he said that their time of sovereignty was now over. It was part of the duty of the saints who followed him that this message should be brought to all humanity, many of whom have been resistant to it up to the present day. There was a tacit admission on the part of the Church that these elemental powers could be brought into the service of Christ in the adoption of so many customs into the Christian ritual. The same can be said of much pagan symbolism. The imagery of Apollo-Helios becomes that of Christ, the Sun of Righteousness. There are several legends that involve the conversion of evil spirits or mythical beings: thus St Creed in Cornwall not only converted a giant to Christianity but also made him throw a great stone

36 *Sampford Courtney.* One of the many Green Men to be found in Devon churches in the neighbourhood of the Woodhenge at Bow, fifteenth century.

37 *Codford St Peter*. The dancing figure brandishing a branch and holding a mallet on a cross shaft fragment in the parish church, 7th century.

in the air and then build her a church on the spot where it fell beside the river Fal. The strength of the past was thus channelled into the purposes of the Faith. Similarly the great black-winged birds that tormented St Patrick during his Lent vigil on the summit of Croagh Patrick were replaced by winged angels come to do him service. A transformation in him brought about a transformation in the elemental forces so that they appeared to him as the messengers of God.

This may explain part of the attraction of the Green Man for the Church. Whether consciously or not, the missionary saints needed to bring the greatest source of living power on earth under the guidance of Christ: the power that is in grass and leaf and sap on which all living things depend. Though they knew that demonic forces dwelt among the works of Nature, they had at the same time to assert the goodness of creation, and there arose a dualism between their fear of the demonic and the beauty and usefulness of God's work. Many years later Dante was to offer a resolution of this dualism by stating that the old gods were in fact angels who, through no fault of their own, were wrongly worshipped by ignorant men.[14]

There was, of course, continued resistance to the Christian attack on the old ways. From the fifth century onwards there are edicts issued by Councils of the Church condemning the worship of trees. They are repeated so frequently presumably because the practice continued. Theodore, Archbishop of Canterbury from 668 to 690, denounced the New Year practice of dressing up as a stag or an old woman.[15] Any who transformed themselves into the appearance of a wild animal had to undergo penance for three years. Charlemagne similarly forbade pagan practices in his capitularies. When, as frequently happened in the course of the invasions of the Dark Ages, the Church and Christian rulers could not protect their subjects, people would return to the old ways because the new faith offered no protection. Thus the archaeological evidence points to a strong revival of native and pagan cults in Britain at the time leading up to the withdrawal of the Roman garrisons and the impact of the Anglo-Saxon invasions, and this may well have been a repeated response at later times of disaster. There would also be another reason for a continued attachment to ancient rituals and ceremonies, and this would be where they particularly related to agriculture and the marking of the seasons. In many cases the Church took over these rituals, as with the blessing of the plough at Rogationtide but, whether or not the Church approved, the rituals had to be performed because they were a means of bonding small communities together and also of educating new generations. Actions ritually performed or marked by ceremonies become memorable: the ritual sets a pattern in the memory for the timing and due sequence of tasks and actions. They impressed on the young essential knowledge of the phases of the moon, of gauging when to plough, when to sow, when to cut the hay, when to scythe the corn and how long to let it stand in stooks, and when to kill the cattle before the winter set in. There are hints of such rituals in a few remains of Dark Age art, such as the figure from part of a cross shaft — thought to be seventh-century — preserved at Codford St Peter (37) in Wiltshire. Here a man dances ecstatically holding a mallet in one hand while brandishing with the other hand the branch of a tree.

There are also indications from legends and chronicles of the survival and continuing force of old beliefs. Thus the prophet Merlin, often described as wearing horns and having power over all beasts, seems to take on many of the characteristics of Cernunnos. As the child of a demon and a nun Merlin crosses the boundaries of pagan and Christian and brings the wisdom of the druids into a new age. Cernunnos may also have survived as the leader of the Wild Hunt, the spectral horsemen who, for example, galloped through the deer park of Peterborough and the woods up to Stamford, as recorded in the Anglo-Saxon Chronicle for 1127.[17] It is a hunt of unbaptized souls riding through woods or across the sky recorded in many parts of Europe. In Scandinavia and Germany the leader of the hunt was Odin or Wotan and in Denmark he was called the Groenjaette (or Green Giant).

The line through which the Green Man assumes his new form in the Dark Ages is not, however, as a survival of an ancient rite or superstition. It is in the context of some of the highest thought and art of the time. The most influential theologian of the Dark Ages, John Scotus Eriugena, who translated Dionysius the Areopagite's works on angels and mysticism into Latin, also wrote of the part played by angels in guiding and maintaining human and mundane affairs. He released and restored great concepts, many of which may later have contributed to the contexts and meanings of the Green Man. He not only presented huge conceptions of the universality of life;[18] he could also show how the major divisions of life are reflected in man. He called man the workshop of all creatures. Man contains the universal creature: he has intellect like an angel, reason like a man, sense like an animal and life like a plant.[19] He therefore has the world of plants within him as the principle of life and growth. Though Scotus compared our mortal body to the broad leaves of the fig in that, as they cast shadows and shut out the rays of the sun, so our bodies cast on the soul the darkness of ignorance and keep out the knowledge of truth — an image that equates flesh with leaves — he also gave new force to the ancient image of the sacred tree by interpreting the Garden of Eden as human nature, in which is planted the Tree of Life. This tree is the word of God and is therefore Christ, 'who is the spiritual bread by which angels and saved humanity, whose conversation is in heaven, are fed'.[20]

Through his writings he gave a new and influential impulse to the Christian Neo-Platonic tradition which was to descend from him to the School of Chartres. According to this line of thought all plant life would take its multitudinous forms from archetypal ideas so that, for example, the Green Man could be understood as the angelic archetype responsible for all vegetation. Such a conception would give a symbolic justification for his incorporation in Christian iconography — and it is a thought we will come to again in discussing the meanings attached to the Green Man in the Middle Ages.

John Scotus came from the Irish culture that did most to preserve the learning and symbolism of the past during the Dark Ages. It was centred on the branch of Western Christianity that achieved the most harmonious balance between what it preserved of the old religion and the teachings of the new faith. It is in Irish sculpture and manuscript illumination that we are most likely to find the Green Man, his antecedents and variants of the foliate head appearing in this period. Thus the figure of Cernunnos is to be seen on the shaft of the North Cross at Clonmacnois (38) and the interlace ornaments illuminated in the Book of Kells and the Book of Durrow are peopled with foliate heads, either of human beings or of beasts, out of which issue the sinuous folds of the lacings or by which they are swallowed up (39).

38 The drawings show (below) Cernunnos on the North Cross at Clonmacnois and (above) a horned figure on a pillar from Cardonagh, also in Ireland. *After Anne Ross, Pagan Celtic Britain, 1967.*

39 An engraving after a disgorging head and snake interlace ornament from the Book of Kells, Trinity College, Dublin. *Mansell Collection*.

It is a sign of archetypal power in an image that it should be capable of transference from one culture to another, from one set of beliefs to a fresh paradigm of faith. This means that it expresses something permanent in the human soul, however much one age may lay different stresses on it from a preceding time. It is this deep permanence that will last as long as man is dependent on the grass of the fields that the Green Man expresses. It may be that as in the case of the Green Man in the Dark Ages an image has to lie largely dormant while changes, more difficult to unravel than the interlacings of the Book of Kells, take place, before its new significances can be seen.

It would also seem that the form of the Green Man as the disgorger and devourer of vegetation first fully evolved in manuscript illuminations in this period of seeming dormancy. The interlace ornament which is one of the most striking features of Irish manuscripts was an introduction from late Roman art and from the Middle East: it may have been brought by those monks from Egypt who are known to have settled in Ireland. They may have brought other traditions: Mlle Henry points to a representation of Christ in the Book of Kells which seems to derive from Osiris.[21] The culture and styles of Irish sacred art were to be carried by missionaries into Great Britain and far across Europe. In their greatest works produced at home, such as the Book of Kells, the Irish monks used the interlace motifs to produce an art that has a concentrated meditative purpose as well as an overwhelming aesthetic effect. To entice the eye to follow their entwinings they used the primal image of the snake, so that the mind in concentrating on the pages was led on a journey that could arouse special states of understanding and consciousness. It was a journey into the mysteries of time and creation, and the secret behind the manifestations of life in the world. It was a journey full of jokes and surprises, which would include the appearance of leaves, of foliate beasts, fishes and wide-eyed men creating their own hair out of the tendrils issuing from their mouths. The Green Man can never be said to be a dominant image in this art: the dominance, except for those pages given to the Apostles or the Virgin, is in the great initial letters or cosmic

40 *Jelling, East Jutland.* The tomb of Harold Bluetooth, died 986, showing the Christ-Odin figure entwined with vegetation. *Mansell Collection.*

patternings that assert themselves as bold emblems out of the infinitesimally fine filaments of which they are formed. Nevertheless it is significant that he appears here in the context of an art whose source is in the profound contemplations of the Irish monks who were the patrons and the artists of this art.

The influence of the Irish artists spread across Europe, and foliate animal heads together with the Green Man frequently appear in manuscripts of the early Middle Ages. Thus the Green Man appears in the Psalter and the Codex made for Egbert, Archbishop of Trier *c.*980, associated with winged serpents or dragons in a style that also shows the influence of Roman scroll decoration.[22]

If the Green Man first arises as the disgorger and devourer of vegetation in the illumination of manuscripts, he returns to sculpture in this new form in association with three of his ancient sources, the cult of the human head, the healing spring and the sacred tree.

In the Norse stories of Odin or Wotan the god sacrificed himself on the World Tree, Yggdrasil, the great ash whose roots are devoured by a dragon. On the tombstone at Jelling in East Jutland of Harold Bluetooth, the first Christian King of Denmark, who died *c.*986, Christ and Odin are merged into one figure with his limbs interlaced with winding branches (40). In some versions of the story this sacrifice enabled Odin to obtain the severed head of a god called Mimir, which he anointed with herbs and kept in a spring

known as the Well of Mimir. By reciting spells over the head he could make it prophesy and tell him many secrets. A strong Celtic influence has been seen in this telling of the story,[23] which links with the many stories that reveal how the Celtic veneration of the head was absorbed into Christian legends — as with the tale of St Denis walking after his decapitation carrying his severed head to Montmartre, or as with St Winifred and her martyrdom and resurrection. The story that best brings together these elements is that of the Cornish or Breton St Melor. He was a young prince whose lands were usurped by his uncle. His uncle persuaded his guardian with bribes to kill St Melor. His guardian cut off the boy's head and set off to show it to St Melor's uncle. On the journey the assassin became ill and weak with thirst and near to death. He cried out for help. The head spoke and told him to plant the staff in the earth. The staff instantly took root and turned into a beautiful tree. The tree put forth branches and fruit and a healing fountain poured from its roots which cured the assassin. Despite this miracle he went to claim his reward. Taken to the top of a hill, he was told to take his choice of the lands he could see. At that moment his eyes dropped from his head. There are several healing wells of St Melor, among them the one at Linkinhorne in Cornwall.[24]

The aura surrounding this cult of the head was ineradicable, and when in the eleventh and twelfth centuries figure sculpture was revived on a grand scale in Christian art the cult gave rise to the series of corbel heads and heads in modillions that ring the exteriors and, sometimes, the interiors of churches. This practice was to give ever more varied opportunities for the Green Man to appear once more in the visual arts.

It was at this time that the Green Man as the disgorger of vegetation first appeared in large numbers in sculpture, and why this took place then must be connected with the revolution affecting the attitude of Western peoples to Nature. In the Dark Ages the Green Man in his older form of the foliate mask went back to his origins in the primal snake and emerged in his new guise with the human face *separated* from the vegetation while being the author and the ruler of it. In the foliate mask human skin and leaf cuticle are inseparable from one another, as though their identity signified the union between human beings and their surroundings that characterized the living experience of men and women in earlier stages of history. What we call tree worship, for example, as though it were a willed choice of faith in a modern sense and as though people then chose to worship trees as someone now might choose to be a Baptist, a Zen Buddhist or a Marxist, was most probably something quite different: it was a natural form of participation with the spirits of groves and forests. The legends of Merlin as the figure linking the old and new worlds are an illustration of this: though his life is devoted to creating the new age of Arthur, in the end he is drawn back into the ancient world of the forest of Broceliande where Nimue either imprisons him or binds him into union with herself in a tree.

That sense of participation lasted long into this century among country people: I think of an old farm labourer who worked for us when I was a boy in the West Country. He walked like a slow-moving oak, and he knew a story about every prominent tree, and every copse, path or field in the immediate neighbourhood: the lane among whose trees a white lady would appear, the drive of a burnt-out manor house up which a black coach drawn

41 *Dijon*. Capital in the crypt of St Bénigne showing a Green Man disgorging vegetation, *c.* 1000.

by galloping headless horses would rush and as suddenly disappear; all told with a deep gurgling enjoyment. We all felt that sense of participation most keenly ourselves on the harvest field as we worked, often against the threat of bad weather, jamming sheaves together to make the stooks, drawing on powers that seemed beyond ourselves, ignoring our aches and bleeding fingers, in an atmosphere of mingled emulation, joy and sadness. Though we no longer 'cried the neck' — the ceremony of saluting the last sheaf, into the neck of which the spirit of the corn or wheat had fled to be preserved until the next season – we knew of it from an old naval captain who worked with us and who had heard it as a boy in a valley of the Tamar on the borders of Devon and Cornwall. There the race to be first to the neck was held betweeen the farms on the sides of the valley. He described how the valley would ring with a shout of 'We've got 'en! We've got 'en!' and from all the other farms would come the ritual question 'What 'ave 'ee got? What 'ave 'ee got?' 'The neck! The neck!' would come the triumphant reply, and the last sheaf would be borne off for the harvest home. Frazer, who also describes similar ceremonies in greater detail, thought that the custom was linked to the melancholy cries of Egyptian reapers at the death of the corn spirit who, to him, was the rustic prototype of Osiris.[25]

Nowadays, sheaves and stooks are largely a matter of the past: the mechanization of farming means that the grain in the ear no longer has to stand its nine dews in the stook. The machines that on today's farms segregate their operators in cabins from direct contact from the soil and what grows on it are one of the distant consequences of the psychic revolution in regard to Nature that began in the Dark Ages. The end of the age of participation in Nature is tentatively heralded by the first appearance of the Green Man as the disgorger and devourer of vegetation on the tomb of St Abre, and then appears fully in the earliest sculpture of the Romanesque period.

The first Green Man I know in sculpture of this period is on a capital in the crypt of St-Bénigne at Dijon (41). Built by Lombard masons in about 1000 for the abbot Volpiano, the crypt is all that survives of a great domed church. His capital stands on a squat column: in the symbolism of the time the column was credited with being a living creature; the veneration that had been paid to trees was transferred to the column. The capital had the meaning and the force of the human head. The energies drawn up from the earth as though they were sap mounting up the column were made explicit in the capital. The rope-like vegetation comes out of the mouth of the Green Man, twisting up round his face and encasing the high leaf that makes his forehead and hair. Coarse and barbaric though he may seem, he will have a great future.

Chapter 4

The Green Man in the Romanesque and Early Gothic Periods

In the south porch of the abbey church of St Pierre at Moissac (42), the tympanum (carved *c.*1130) shows Christ in majesty as described by St John in Revelation, surrounded by the four beasts of the evangelists and the twenty-four elders. Christ is supported by two angels. The two outer bands of the tympanum are richly carved with vegetation. The Christ is a powerful, frightening lord or king whose garments are vibrant with cosmic power. The beasts of the evangelists symbolize not only the four gospels but the four elements and the four temperaments of man which are made complete in the human nature of Christ. Their bodies twist with extraordinary energies as though the power of Christ at once attracts their gaze and drives them outwards. The crowned elders gaze in wonder at the revelation of God in Man. The rounded design is bordered by an unfolded ribbon or meander pattern which issues from a beast head on the right of Christ and crosses up and over to the up-ended head of a horned Cernunnos on His left (43).

The lintel beneath the tympanum carries ten roundels of thistle-like rosettes issuing from the mouths of two beasts on either side, each snouted like the beast head in the tympanum from whose mouth issues the ribbon surround. The thistle pattern continues down the trumeau or central pillar dividing the two doors and is visible between the crossover pattern made by the carvings of three pairs of lions and lionesses. It is on one side of this trumeau

42 *Moissac*. From the south porch of the abbey church of St Pierre: the tympanum of Christ surrounded by the beasts of the Evangelists and the 24 Elders, before 1130. The ribbon ornament runs from the mouth of a beast (left) to a Cernunnos head (right; see fig. 43).

43 *Moissac*. The Cernunnos head disgorging the ribbon which encloses the semicircle of the judgment in the tympanum.

that can be seen the famous figure of Jeremiah as the dancing prophet. The outer sides of the doors are deeply scalloped. There are further carvings in the porch, of which the outer surround consists of panels of foliate heads disgorging vegetation. Though most of this surround has been recut, it follows the pattern of original work on the right-hand side of the porch. Many of these heads have the horned Cernunnos features of the head in the tympanum on the left of Christ (44).

What is the Green Man doing here in his old unregenerate form as Cernunnos or, in what must be a related form, the beast head that disgorges foliage? It could be argued that the head in the tympanum is that of the Devil and that what comes out of his mouth is ribbon rather than foliage. There is a deliberate similarity between him and the foliate heads on the outer side of the porch, just as there is a deliberate similarity between the beast head in the tympanum which complements the Cernunnos head and the beasts of the lintel. His appearance here raises many questions, but the main point to note is that Moissac shows him already established in one of the key iconographical settings of a church, the porch with its associated carvings, and it establishes him in a place of honour of which we shall see many more examples.

Moissac lies on one of the pilgrim routes to Compostela. It was a priory of the Cluniac Order, in the realms of which many of the most notable Green Men of this period are to be found. Strong influences from Moorish Spain have been seen in this porch, in the scalloped door surrounds, in the attitudes of the elders which are derived from illustrations of Islamic musicians, and even in the representation of Christ which has been compared to an Ummayad prince holding court in his diwan.[1] It is known that many Muslim craftsmen and architects worked in Christian Europe in this period, and the sudden change in the standards of cutting masonry stone which begins from around 1100 has been attributed to the influence of these craftsmen with their superior techniques. That this porch at Moissac and several other great churches should bear the mark of contact with the feared religion and culture of Islam should be seen as a right of great conquests, the conquests that had won back Toledo in 1085 and the Holy Land together with Jerusalem in 1099. The Christ at Moissac, as with the even more powerful Christ at Vézelay who is shown spreading the Word among all nations, expresses the dominating power and expansive force of a Western Europe that was full of confidence and energy.

The Moissac porch is a masterwork of the late Romanesque: its themes and moods were shortly to be transformed by an aesthetic revolution comparable in importance to the psychic revolution in man's attitude to Nature described in the last chapter. This aesthetic revolution, which could not have come about without that earlier change, was the rise of the Gothic style, in which the Green Man image was to undergo most notable transformations. He was prepared for that over a period of the 150 years of the development of the Romanesque style during which he came out of the borders of the manuscripts in which he had undergone a secret transformation during the Dark Ages to appear in more vital form with the revival of three-dimensional sculptural figurations.

The Romanesque style arises in response to the new era that began for Central and North-Western Europe as the attacking races of the Vikings and the Magyars were either contained or themselves absorbed into the Catholic culture and religion of the West. Further south the tide was beginning to turn against the Muslims in Spain and in Provence. In many parts, particularly along the Loire, the successful organization of resistance to the invaders at a local level had led to the introduction of feudal institutions often centred on the supreme technological invention of the period, the castle. An increase in population led not only to the revival of trade and of town life but to the need to clear forests and cultivate virgin land. The people of Europe began to expand, first over their own regions, and then by the end of the century they were ready for the great adventure of the Crusades.

It was a time of hope and in this period the Green Man starts to return. Romanesque architecture is the greatest evidence of this new urge to expand. Men began to build again on a great scale because they could afford to do so and because, in general, it was worth while constructing stone churches that would not be destroyed before they were completed.

The style became linked with important political and religious movements. It was adopted as the official art of the Ottonian Emperors and was to be so identified with the Holy Roman Empire that Romanesque architecture survived in Germany and Italy longer than anywhere else. The style also was identified with the Reform movement in the Church, led most notably and in its most civilizing aspects by the abbots and monks of Cluny.

Figurative sculpture of the earlier Romanesque is comparatively rare and, apart from that in the crypt of St-Bénigne, we have come across few Green Men heads carved in stone from the first part of the eleventh century. This is not to say they were not carved: they could well have been replaced by the greater riches of late Romanesque sculpture. Before discussing the Green Man as he appeared in this later sculpture it is necessary to say more about the general context of Romanesque architecture in which he appeared.

The sculpture of Romanesque churches, where there were schools of sculptors to patronize and money to pay for them, is concentrated on the capitals, the corbels and modillions, and the doorways. The plastered surfaces of the walls, vaults and wooden ceilings also allowed opportunities for paintings. The painting in some churches, such as St-Savin in Poitou, has survived to a remarkable extent, giving one a warm impression of the grandeur and richness of the interiors. Between the calm in the atmosphere of Romanesque churches, given out by the piers and columns, the rounded arches, the carved apses and the deep wide crypts, on the one hand, and the vigour and violence of the subjects in the carvings, on the other hand, there is sometimes an extraordinary contrast. The monsters who attack one another or devour man possess an official reason for being there: they exemplify the passions and desires that man must overcome in himself if he is to find salvation. Art, however, is complex in its origins as in its meanings. These carvings, nightmares issuing into awareness in the stillness of these churches, reflect the struggle for existence of man in a hostile environment. They are a reflection on the horrors and fears of life in the Dark Ages; they are an acknowledgement of the terrors of the past that have had to be overcome.

But even in sculptures as early and as seemingly barbaric as those of the crypt of St-Bénigne, there is an urge to express something new through the capital as the voice of the energies in the column. This is to be seen in all the attempts to copy or to perform variations on the theme of the Roman acanthus capital. It was as though the sculptors felt the column was the trunk

44 *Moissac*. Foliate heads on the outer jambs of the south porch. Turn the page sideways to see the horned Cernunnos head.

63

of a tree that had to be made to burst into leaf. Though their masters and patrons were telling them to portray the consequences of tasting the Tree of Knowledge of Good and Evil, what in their innermost hearts they wished to do was to recreate the Tree of Life.

By the end of the eleventh century they were increasingly finding the skills to introduce more and more figures into their capitals, frequently telling stories or making moral points in images that were surrounded by vegetation. Beast heads sprout vegetation or spring out of leaves as though they were surprising fruits. The volutes of capitals arch into the single heads of monsters with two bodies. Centaurs gallop in and out of woodland. Demons appear to torture the damned. And among all the leaves and interlaced fronds the Green Man returns in a damburst of imagery, the origins of which have been traced to the Great Mother imagery of the Neolithic and subsequent periods, to Mesopotamia, Scythia and the steppes of Russia, Coptic Egypt, Armenia, Georgia, Syria, Scandinavia and the Celtic regions, which all contributed themes to the basic Roman tradition, made familiar from the carvings and buildings of the imperial and colonial past of Rome.

The Green Man is only one of tens and hundreds of images competing for the attention of Romanesque sculptors. Licensed to portray sin in all its forms, symbolically through the struggles of wild and mythical beasts and through the devouring of man by the beast in him, the sculptors attacked the stone with gusto. The influential scholar Hrabanus Maurus (784-856) had identified the leaf with sin, especially with sexual sin, and this probably gave a further licence to the portrayal of vegetation.[2] Though passages such as this may have licensed the artists in their choice of subjects, the artists were also inspired to emulate and to perform their own variations on the innumerable remains and fragments of pagan and early Christian art, in which vegetation themes and the peopled scroll would figure so widely. The effect of

the tradition of the peopled scroll is to be seen not only in sculptured stone but in metalwork as well. Thus in the candlesticks of Bishop Bernward in Hildesheim from the beginning of the Romanesque period[3] and in the Gloucester Candlestick (now in the Victoria and Albert Museum) from near its end, we find beautiful designs of interlaced foliage with the bodies of human beings struggling or striving upwards. The flames that glowed once on these candlesticks symbolized eternal light and it is towards this that the figures are striving out of the dark wood of sin. In the Gloucester Candlestick certain figures have escaped and sit round the foot, resting like swimmers who have narrowly escaped from drowning. Works of art such as these indicate a changing attitude to the meaning of vegetation: they suggest a more detached view than that given in interpretations such as that of Hrabanus Maurus. They seem to say, 'Life is like that: it is a struggle against entanglements of desire and the flesh; but the very branches and leaves which threaten to bind you are also the means appointed for your triumphal climb to the light.' The close analogy between man's sexual nature and the writhing vegetation is made even clearer in some of the carved colonnettes which are completely covered with scenes of naked men and women caught in vegetation and which are to be found, for example, on the west fronts of Chartres and of Lincoln (64 and 49).

49 *Lincoln*. Man caught in the coils of vegetation: carving on a column of the west front of the cathedral, *c*. 1140.

These are tame when compared with the many examples of exhibitionist figures or of couples or individuals indulging in a variety of sexual practices in Romanesque churches in Spain, France and the British Isles. Male and female figures display their genitalia often grossly exaggerated, couples copulate or indulge in homosexual practices. In numbers of examples these figures are associated with vegetation and are interspersed with heads or, more rarely, figures of Green Men.

The surface reason why these figures were carved in churches seems to have been for purposes of moral instruction. The most influential patrons of Romanesque sculpture were the abbots and monks of monastic institutions. They had their obvious reasons for teaching the deplorable effects of concupiscence, and many and horrifying are the denunciations of woman and of lust in their writings. They needed the artist to reinforce the message of the dangers of sexual desires and, through their authority, the images depicting the ugly nature of these desires and the punishments awaiting those who surrendered to them were carved for the instruction of ordinary people inside and outside churches.

One of the most widely found images is the figure of the Sheela-na-Gig, or naked woman displaying her parts (45). She appears in the period from 1080 onwards, at a time when the Green Man is increasing in popularity. Though it has been denied that there is any evidence for linking her with any earlier cult or surviving folk custom,[4] I think that, whatever the moral justification the clerics may have devised for her representation in churches, she is one of the many indications that the archetype of the Great Mother was stirring in the dreams and thoughts of men. Another authority[5] identifies the Sheela-na-Gig with the Morrigan in her role as the Celtic war goddess; she appears to heroes as a hag but when they consent to make love to her turns into a beautiful woman. In Irish mythology she becomes the lover of the Dagda, the great comic god who may also have contributed to the evolution of the Green Man. At Rath Blaic in Ireland there is a Romanesque window

48 *opposite*. *Marburg*. The Green Man as the utterer of the Word: one of many Green Men on the pulpitum of the Elisabethskirche, *c*. 1340.

50 *Brioude*. These women
half-figures face the men
in fig. 51 across the nave
of the church.

sill in which a Green Man is carved beside what seems to be a Sheela-na-Gig.[6]
On the twelfth-century font of the church of Winterbourne Monkton, just
north of the centre of matriarchal worship of earlier times at Avebury, there
is carved among a bold patterning of chevrons, which are a signature of
the Great Goddess, the figure of a naked woman with her legs splayed as
she gives birth to a spray of vegetation (46).[7]

Elsewhere I have pointed out that the patterns used frequently in Northern
Romanesque architecture — the lozenge, chevron and spiral, as in Durham
Cathedral — go back to the Megalithic carvings made in honour of the Great
Mother.[8] The most likely mode of transmission for these symbols is through
their use in the weaving of corn dollies at harvest time. It is also possible
that people continued to carve the earthy image of the Sheela-na-Gig for
their fertility and seasonal rituals. In addition to their appearance in churches
as a warning against sexual temptation, they also symbolized fertility and,
like the Celtic image of the severed head, they acted as guardians against
evil. The displaying of the sexual parts was popularly thought to put the
Devil to flight. A less startling warning against lust was provided by the
siren or mermaid with her tail divided at the crutch. In rare and beautiful

51 *Brioude*. The complementary male figures to those in fig. 50.

examples at Chanteuges and Brioude in the Auvergne we find a transformation of the theme in which the form of the temptress from the sea is changed into a half figure of vegetation. Male as well as female figures are carved with their twin tails ending in leafage. At Brioude (50 and 51) the male and female capitals face one another across the nave and also there is an extraordinary carving of a naked man whose legs turn into twisting branches with leaves.

Whatever the reasons ecclesiastics gave for allowing the Sheela-na-Gig to appear in their churches, there is a much deeper significance in the return of the Great Mother into sacred art. It is, I think, extraordinary that the Great Mother and her son, lover, guardian, the Green Man should both return in this same period. It may be that a similar process is taking place today: just as the rise of feminism has been accompanied, through quite independent lines of research, by the rediscovery of the dominant matriarchal religions of ancient Europe, so it may be that the Green Man is stirring again because in the deep ecology of the spirit he is linked to her as part of the same web of myth.

The Sheela-na-Gig was a potent reminder of the Goddess in her ancient form. She appears also in a new and profoundly influential way as the Virgin.

The Black Virgins of the eleventh and twelfth centuries, contemporary with the revival of the Green Man, also owe much to the past — to depictions of the Gallo-Roman deity, the Magna Mater, and also to the influence of the Isis cult so widespread in the Roman Empire. The ancient significances of the Goddess with her son Horus and mourning her dead lover Osiris from whose body sprouts the wealth of the earth returned in a new mode to inspire devotion in a Christian context.

Not only were the early images of the Virgin and Child derived from those of Isis with the child Horus seated on her lap, but several of the churches where Black Virgins are still present or were formerly venerated are built near or on the ruins of temples of Isis. The original Black Virgin of Le Puy may also have been a statue of Isis.[9] Here it would seem to be a case, not of the secret survival of the ancient Egyptian religion, but of a natural transference of the attributes and supremacy of one aspect of the Great Goddess to another — even to the appearance of the child Horus in a new form, the Christ Child. If we include Set in the new context as the Devil, then where is Osiris, the god from whose body sprouts the vegetation of the Nile and whose face when he judges in the underworld is green? Can it be the archetypal Osiris who reappears at this time as the Green Man, now rarely shown with his body, but with vegetation pouring out of his mouth?

Or is he Attis reborn? There are even more sites of the Black Virgin which were once sacred to Cybele. Her statue in Rome showed a black stone where her head should be and her great festival took place on 25 March, later to become Lady Day. Or is he Adonis? The Black Virgin of Montserrat stands on what was once a temple of Venus-Aphrodite. Or is he all these because he must return with the force of spring whenever his Goddess returns?

Miracles attended the Black Virgins. Though to modern researchers their statues are for the most part carvings of the later eleventh and twelfth centuries, their legendary origins are nearly always much earlier. Some are the work of St Luke the artist evangelist who also carved the Santo Volto of Lucca. Some appeared miraculously in caves. Notre-Dame de Boulogne arrived at her home in a boat without sails or oars, accompanied only by a copy of the Gospels in Syriac, while King Dagobert was at mass. Many examples of the Black Virgin, however, first revealed themselves in trees as though, in another form of transference from an older religion to a new faith, she issued from the tree cults of the past.

There is another link between the Black Virgins and many representations of the Green Man in this period. All the ancient Black Virgins I have seen have a numinous and hieratic calm, as with the Virgin of Notre-Dame d'Espoir in Dijon (52). She is the manifestation of a level of being and experience infinitely beyond human failings and sufferings and it is, perhaps, precisely because she possesses this freedom from misery that she is able to comfort and to bless through her presence. The atmosphere she generates is the evidence that there is, in truth, a level of peace that is attainable and is full of succour for human griefs and hopes. Many of the Green Men possess something of her calm and independence of the vicissitudes of ordinary mortals. Though the Green Man appears among the violent and frightening monsters and demons, in many examples I have seen of the later Romanesque period there is a stillness in his portrayals, as he gets on calmly with his job of providing the earth with vegetation, that makes a striking contrast

to what his neighbours are doing. Thus the Green Man is to be seen as one of the jamb capitals at Kilpeck beside the Tree of Life carved in the tympanum of the doorway (15). At Aulnay there is a magnificent plump-cheeked Green Man giving out the same feeling of calm and peaceful endeavour (55).

This is not to say that the old associations were played down. At Schwäbisch-Gmünd Cernunnos is carved on a capital complete with horns and snakes coming out of his mouth. At San Pietro in Toscania, Viterbo, one of the most remarkable sculptures incorporating the Green Man shows him twice as a three-headed or tricephalic deity: the lower tricephalos rises from a torso and he holds a snake (53). The vegetation proceeds as peopled scrolls from the lower tricephalos up to the horned tricephalos set above the window framed by the vegetation and down again in a cycle of growth. There is a startling ferocity in these faces which is at odds with the beauty of the scrolled vegetation that issues from them. Mrs Basford sees these tricephaloi as unmistakably demonic and points to the tradition drawn from the Apocryphal Gospel of Nicodemus in which Christ at the Harrowing of Hell addresses 'three-headed Beelzebub'.[10] It was with three heads that Dante was to depict Satan at the centre of the earth. It was a theme from antiquity[11] to be played with by Gothic as well as Romanesque sculptors. Both would use it as well to signify the exact opposite of Satan: the Trinity. There is another interpretation, which is that these heads represent the sources and devourers of time and all its works. I am struck as well by another feeling that is not wicked, though it appears in the expression of anger. I would call it the anger of artistic impatience — the exasperation that the artist and the forces of the earth must share at the baulking of the longing to express everything that is within them.

Something of the same anger is to be seen in the profile faces of Green Men in the doorway of the church of St-Michel d'Aigulhe perched high on one of the peaks of Le Puy. They are placed on either side of the tympanum (57). They look like horned and ferocious Roman emperors glaring at the rich leafage (54), in which birds play, that curves round from one mouth to the other. They are set within a three-cusped arch that would seem to derive directly from Islam. The centre cusp shows the Lamb of God with elders adoring in the side cusps. In the spandrels of the outer cusps are yet more Green Men, this time full face but also with vegetation in which birds play issuing from their mouths. What is most extraordinary is that squatting on top of these Green Men are two naked men, their sex hidden or replaced by scrolls of foliage. They hold the foliage on either side of them as though they are in control of it. It is as though they signify men who are aware of their sexual nature and also know how to master it without letting it destroy the great energies within them. A head, expressing similar calm and radiance, is set in the foliage of one of the capitals (56).

These figures announce a theme to which we will come again in the Gothic period: the observer and guide who appears out of vegetation and who will be a transformation of the message of the Green Man.

This is a culmination of a process to be found frequently in Romanesque sculpture. It is a reverse of the metamorphoses of classical legends in which men and women are transformed into beasts, birds or plants. Here the plants grow into animals or human heads. It is like an unconscious criticism of the doctrines that equated the leaves of plants with the entanglements of sin. It is a feature to be found, for example, in the capitals of Autun where

53 *Toscanella*. Tricephalic heads giving out and swallowing peopled scrolls: from the west front of San Pietro, 12th century. *Alinari-Giraudon*.

55 *opposite. Aulnay*. A disgorging Green Man on the exterior of the apse, 12th century.

54 *Le Puy*. A Green Man at the base of the tympanum surround.

56 *Le Puy*. The Green Man as the fruit or flower of vegetation.

57 *Le Puy*. The door and tympanum of St Michel d'Aigulhe, with disgorging foliate heads and human figures rising out of vegetation, 12th century.

bear heads or cat heads grow out of the vegetation, or at Saulieu where there is a capital on which the fronds all end in animal or human heads. The transformation is to be seen also at Le Mans (58) and in remarkable stiff-leaf capitals at Sées of the early Gothic period. At Sées some of the capitals are entirely stiff-leaf, knobbed like young bracken sprouts: some have turned into bright, intelligent human faces; while in the choir there is one capital entirely studded with human heads. Such sculptures hint at ideas for which some parallels can be found in contemporary thought, both in writings of the School of Chartres — to which we will come later — and in the tendency, noted by Marie-Madeleine Davy, in writers of the time to hint at a relationship between man and Nature.[12] Here man has a salvatory role where the rest of Nature is concerned. Through man's own salvation, brought about by the Incarnation, the beasts, birds, creatures and plants of earth will also share in the process of redemption. It is possible that the emergence of this new form of the Green Man is a reflection of this line of thought appearing frequently, even if not in the prominent positions he was to occupy during the flowering of the concept in the Gothic period.

Thus at Notre-Dame de Poitiers (*c*.1145) we find his faces in a frieze on the elaborately carved west front dividing the line of apostles from the sculptures depicting the Fall and the Redemption. They wait and they witness and they merely watch the figures and their dramas. But their influence is to be seen on one battered carving which is the head of Jesse, the tree of whose genealogy comes out of his head rather than from his loins as in the iconography first devised at St-Denis and made most famous by the Jesse window at Chartres.

Here the Green Men are to be seen in the context of the Creation, Fall and Redemption of man, of which we will give several later examples. The theme of the sacred tree appears here in the Tree of the Knowledge of Good

and Evil. Among the stories linked together in the Legend of the True Cross was that of the death of Adam. According to the Gospel of Nicodemus Adam, when close to death, sent his son Seth into Paradise to ask for a branch of the Tree of Mercy to ease his last moments. In most versions the angels refused this request, but in others Seth not only returned with the branch but placed it in his father's mouth. The tree then grew from Adam's body in the ground.[13] By the time of the writing of the *Golden Legend* in the thirteenth century this Tree of Mercy growing from Adam's grave had become identical with the tree of the Cross. Also in this version of the story Seth placed three seeds of the Tree of Mercy in his father's mouth and these seeds grew into three trees standing on his grave. These trees provided the wood for the Cross.[14] What I find so striking in this story is the image of Adam with the branch in his mouth and the resemblance here with the Green Man as the disgorger of vegetation and the medium for the works of time. There is a redemptive feeling in this story which counters the identification of the leaf with sin. It also relates to the hidden mystery of the intelligence underlying natural forms, of which I see the Green Man in his fruit or flower form as the emblem.

The Green Man in the Romanesque and Early Gothic Periods

58 *opposite. Le Mans.* Heads arising from acanthus leaves on a nave capital, *c.* 1160.

The fullest expression of the idea I find implicit in these fruit or flower Green Men is not from Christian writings but from the works of the Sufi saint and mystic Mevlana Jalalu'ddin Rumi. In one of his poems in the *Diwani Shamsi Tabrizi* he describes the process of the awakening of consciousness through all the levels of materiality

> Conceive the Soul as a fountain, and these created things as rivers
> While the fountain flows, the rivers run from it.
> Put grief out of your mind and keep quaffing this river-water;
> Do not think of the water failing; for this water is without end.
> From the moment you came into the world of being,
> A ladder was placed before you that you might escape.
> First you were mineral, later you turned to plant,
> Then you became animal: how should this be a secret to you?
> Afterwards you were made man, with knowledge, reason, faith;
> Behold the body, which is a portion of the dust-pit, how perfect it has grown!
> When you have travelled on from man, you will doubtless become an angel.[15]

That was written in the thirteenth century, long after the first major contacts with Islam following the Crusades, but it expresses an idea already deeply founded in Sufi thought. There is another tradition from Islam which may have influenced the thoughts of the masons and carvers, coming into contact as they did with Muslim craftsmen and architects whose superior skills they were eager to emulate and to learn from. This is the story of Khidr (mentioned earlier in connexion with St George on p.29). There are legends of him in which, like Osiris, he is dismembered and reborn; and prophecies connecting him, like the Green Man, with the end of time. His name means the Green One or the Verdant One, he is the voice of inspiration to the true aspirant and committed artist. He can come as a white light or the gleam on a blade of green grass, but more often as an inner mood. The sign of his presence is the ability to work or to experience with tireless enthusiasm beyond one's

59 *Mainz*. Christ in Judgment in the tympanum of the west door of the cathedral. There are six Green Men in the foliage surround, *c*. 1210. *Kathleen Basford*.

60 *opposite*. *Chartres*. The Royal Portal showing Christ in Majesty and the column statues, *c*. 1150. There are some forty heads rising out of the foliage surrounds to each tympanum.

normal capacities. In this there may be a link across the cultures, because one reason for the enthusiasm of the medieval sculptors for the Green Man may be that he was to them the symbol of their source of inspiration.

Though it is pure conjecture to see the influence of the story of Khidr on the subsequent development of the Green Man, what is not conjecture is the influence of Islam on the rapid development of the Gothic style from the 1130s onwards, most notably in the introduction of the pointed arch from Muslim North Africa, first into Burgundian Romanesque as at Autun and then into the new Gothic choir which Abbot Suger was building at St-Denis. This was to bring about the expression of new conceptions of space and light that were themselves the expression of new understandings of the range of divine and human thought and of the relationship of man to Nature. Through the introduction of these conceptions the Green Man was to undergo a further transformation and fuller acceptance into Christian imagery.

There was much artistically and theologically in the image that needed to be resolved. If we take his newer form, the human head disgorging vegetation, then why does he perform an act that is against Nature? What is the source of the vegetation that comes out of him? One interpretation of him says that he is related to two other figures familiar in carvings of the time. These are the grinning giant who pulls his mouth open, and the tongue protruder. It is said that these represent three stages in the utterance of the Word: the first being the opening of the mouth, the second the showing of the tongue, and the third the transformation of the tongue into foliage as the Logos.[17] There is in fact a sequence of heads at Milly-la-Forêt near Dijon which do this. But why in so many instances, as at Moissac, is the utterer of foliage given the horns of the Devil or of Cernunnos? Why, when the Church had been at such pains to eradicate tree worship or to incorporate the veneration of the tree in the symbolism of the Church, was the old god of the forests allowed not only to take his place in churches and cathedrals,

61 *Chartres*. Detail
showing the heads in the
foliage surround to the
central tympanum.

62 *opposite. Vendôme*. The
Green Man takes to the
skies on the tower of the
Abbey of St-Trinité, *c.*
1170. See figure 63.

but to be seen as the author of the vegetation on which men depended for
their subsistence? And why, moreover, does he appear, whether horned or
not, so often close to representations of Christ on the tympana of porches
and entrances; each of which exemplified Christ's words, 'I am the door'?
Thus he is to be seen in leaf-mask form in the tympana of doors of the Rhineland cathedrals of Mainz (57) and Worms. There was an unconscious Mani-
chaeism in the attitude to the works of Nature here: on the one hand, they
are the creation of God and therefore intrinsically good; and on the other
hand, they are the symbols of sin and lust and therefore irredeemably bad.
It was the task of the Gothic Masters to rescue the works of creation from
this last imputation, and one of the means by which they achieved this was
to develop further the third category of the Green Man, the head — and
sometimes the body as well, as at Le Puy — of a man as the flower or fruit
of vegetation.

The place where this transformation can best be seen is Chartres. It is also
the place where many of the themes in this chapter can be seen brought
together. According to legend it was the holiest place in Gaul, the druid

63 *Vendôme*. The Green Man on the tower in figure 62 with a harpy above him.

shrine of the *Virgo Paritura*, the virgin who is to give birth. It possessed an ancient healing well, now contained within the crypt. It had possessed since 876 the sacred relic of the shift Mary had worn when giving birth to Christ. It possessed in addition one of the most revered of all Black Virgins. From the tenth century onwards it was one of the most renowned centres of learning in Europe; there the Christian Neo-Platonic tradition was particularly treasured and enriched. The school reached the height of its fame under Thierry of Chartres as chancellor in the middle of the twelfth century. Two other writers who probably studied at Chartres, Bernard Sylvester and Alan of Lille, both expressed in Neo-Platonic terms new ideas about the nature, creation, and origins of man. Bernard wrote a parable[18] describing the creation of man as the culmination of a process for which all Nature had been in travail through all the preliminary work of making the elements, heaven and earth, and the plants and animals. Alan of Lille in his *Anticlaudianus* tells how Nature, to set right the ills of earth 'and to grant us solace for the damage we have done',[19] wishes to create a perfect man. Though she can make the body she cannot form the soul, and Prudence at her behest travels to heaven where she requests such a soul from God. God assents and she returns to Nature with the gift of the soul imbued with every virtue. The new man is made and the forces of evil rise up to do battle with him. They are discomfited and the realm of Nature is made fruitful as never before. It is in Alan's assertion of the need of Nature for perfection in humanity, and for the world of plants to achieve a corresponding perfection, that we can see an expression of the salvatory role mentioned earlier. Because the perfect man has come into existence, earth is the rival of heaven; there is no need of the plough to wound the earth; trees and vines no longer need pruning; they all bring forth without labour. Both writers seem to be voicing in words the feelings of the earlier sculptors who had found the heads of beasts and humans growing out of the leaf capitals as they carved them.

Thierry of Chartres is thought to have planned the iconography of the West or Royal Portal of Chartres in collaboration with the master sculptor, whose name is unknown. Its theme is the universality of all knowledge under the guidance of Christ, who is set in the central tympanum of the three doors (60). The Virgin is given a new prominence here as she is shown over the south door in her aspect as Sapientia, or Heavenly Wisdom. The north tympanum shows the Ascension of Christ. Beside all three doors stand the famous column statues of the Royal Portal, men and women of the Old Testament, kings, queens, prophets and prophetesses, in the carving of which a new understanding of the individuality of human beings was given to the world for the first time. They represent the union and balance between priesthood and kingship, *sacerdotium* and *regnum*. Every portion of the doorways and their surrounds is richly carved, patterned, historiated, and enriched, whether with the Labours of the Months, the signs of the Zodiac, the events of the lives of Mary and of Christ, or with sages, philosophers, angels and elders. All these have been annotated and argued over by scholars for years, but not one hitherto unexplained sequence in the sculpture. This is to be seen in the bands of foliage that form the outermost surrounds of the three arches. Arising out of the foliage are the heads of some forty-four men (61). Admittedly they have largely been recut, but they would appear to replace accurately the worn and weatherbeaten originals. They are at once the joyous witnesses and the consequences of the great transforming events of Christ's Incarnation, Ascension, and Second Coming which they frame. They exemplify the Green Man as the fruit or flower of vegetation, here flourishing in all the benefits of the universal knowledge radiating from Christ. There are similar bands of foliage surrounding the tympana of Moissac and Vézelay, to give only two earlier examples, but these are merely formal patterns based on the acanthus leaf. They are not developed into a further level of awareness. Furthermore, these heads at Chartres make an infinitely more lively pattern: the leaves curl out from each head as though they were foliate angel wings, making a rising and falling rhythm to flow round the arches.

Here too the theme of the Green Man is advanced to a new prominence. From being part of a cast of imagery to be seen in capitals, corbels or tympana he becomes a starting point or focus for architectural as well as sculptural design. What I mean by this can be seen even more clearly a few miles south of Chartres in the superb single-spired tower of the Abbey of Ste-Trinité at Vendôme. The abbey here was celebrated for its possession of a rare and wonderful relic: one of the tears of Christ. The wealth accrued from pilgrims coming to venerate this relic paid in the 1170s for the building of this tower, which is directly influenced by the greatest of all works of early Gothic architecture, the south-west tower of Chartres itself. The tower at Vendôme is built with great angle buttresses at each of its four corners. Halfway up the tower the buttresses facing the square are carved with the immense head of a Green Man (62 and 63). These faces articulate, and give expression to, the energies rising up the buttresses that help to make this one of the first declarations of the soaring vertical aspirations of the Gothic style. And as the stone rose even higher in future buildings, so the Green Man would rise with it, to look down on, to brood on, or smile at the towns and countryside around where once his ancestors had been honoured in the mystery religions or revered as the gods of farming and of the forests.

64 *Chartres*. A man rises up triumphantly through the vegetation on a colonnette of the Royal Portal.

Chapter 5

The Triumph of the Green Man in the Gothic Period

If you have so much of the Green Man in your nature that you enjoy being out in the rain, and if you are lucky enough to be at Chartres during a heavy and continuous downpour, you will see something remarkable. Not only will you watch the stones of the cathedral deepen in tone to mysterious combinations of browny-orange and blue-greys with hints of green and note the glistening of walls and buttresses where the angled rain is beaten against the surfaces and streams down to shine on the outer columns of the portals and to revivify the flat carvings of plants and foliage, but you will feel the great building respond as though it were a huge plant that needed rain for the spatial marvels of its recesses, arches, gables, tabernacles and flying buttresses to reveal yet more of their mysteries. The way in which the masters of Chartres provided for the run-off from their cathedral is a fascinating study in itself: they counted on there being sun and light enough to illumine the colours of their windows; they took advantage of the fact that the cathedral lies not on a true setting to the east but is skewed to the north to arrange that there should be special effects of lighting on significant days — for example the statue of John the Baptist in the North Portal is only reached by the setting sun around his day of 24 June (70) — and in a smaller but still fascinating way they made the rain serve a symbolic purpose as well.

This is to be seen when the water pouring down the façades of the transepts is guided by hidden conduits to issue out of the spandrels of the North and South Portals (65 and 66) through the mouths of beasts, jetting in curving gouts that resemble the flying buttresses above, to splash on the steps below. The North Portal is devoted among its themes to the Virgin, her genealogy, and the foretellers of Christ together with the story of Creation, and the arts and sciences. The South Portal is devoted to the risen Christ, the doctors, saints and martyrs of the Church, and to the moral virtues and their antitheses. One of the overall symbols of the ground plan of the cathedral is that of the cross; the transepts form the cross-bar and signify the line of time, north to south, transecting the line of eternity which runs east to west along the choir and nave. This symbolism is important for what follows.

Nearly everything about the design of these portals invites you inwards — the stairs, the porticoes, the recessing of the statues to each of the triple doors — to draw you into the cathedral. The only elements in the spatial and sculptural design to project outwards are these gargoyle beast heads and the sculptures that support them. In the case of three of the four beast heads the supporting sculptures are those of triplets of heads of the Green Man (68). The odd one out (on the South Portal) is supported by three animal heads — an ox, a lion, and a ram (67). As the gargoyle heads are supported

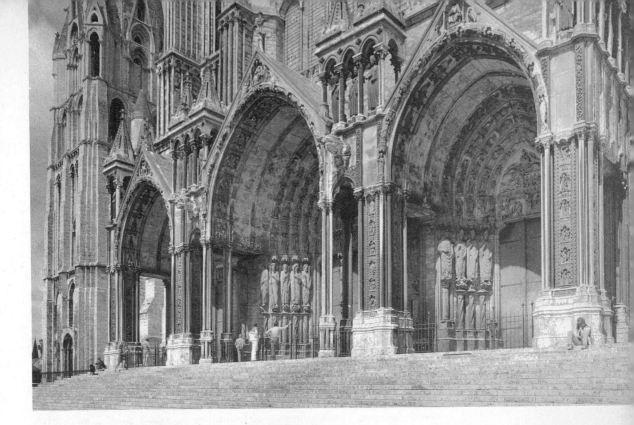

65 *Chartres*. The south transept portal, *c*. 1210, showing the gargoyle beastheads projecting on either side of the central door.

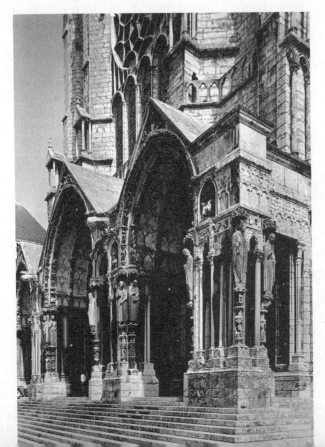

66 *Chartres*. The north transept portal, *c*. 1210, showing beasthead gargoyles similar to those on the south portal.

by the Green Men or the beast heads, so these in turn are corbelled out on brackets carved with the wavy motion that is the convention in Gothic sculpture for representing water or a flood. The overall symbolism seems to be clear: the earthly waters that pour on the cathedral are transformed into the waters of life as the devout seeker, having undergone transformation through witnessing the mysteries and marvels of the interior, goes out to the world, making his or her dealings in life fruitful with the blessings of the waters of life.

Waters pour out of the heads of the beasts as leaves pour out of the mouths of two of the Green Men on the South Portal. Every commentator on Chartres is convinced that all the sculptures form part of an overall iconographic scheme in which each detail was agreed between the clergy and the sculptors. Apart from Mrs Basford,[1] hardly anyone mentions these Green Men and no one, as far as I am aware, has tried to relate them to the overall scheme despite the fact that their inclusion must have been as much a matter for discussion between patrons and carvers as any other feature of the portals.

These three Green Man heads on the South Portal set a pattern, I believe, for the future development in Europe of the image. Just as the column statues standing behind them marked a further stage onwards from those of the Royal Portal in conveying a new sense of the individuality of the soul — which was to be followed at Rheims and elsewhere — so these Green Men in their human characteristics have acquired a new individuality of expression. Furthermore, the leaves that issue from them are in each case recognizable as those of particular species: they are the oak, the acanthus and the vine. To understand the significance of finding recognizable plant species here, we have to go back sixty or seventy years to the first appearance of the Gothic style at St-Denis. There the theme of associating vegetation with sin underwent a transformation as the sculptors undertook a purer copying of classical models. At Sens, the next great centre of early Gothic, the capitals are carved with simple and beautiful ideal plant shapes that suggest a similarity with the art of Ancient Egypt or, as though under the influence of Neo-Platonic thought, they were meant to signify the eternal ideas of vegetation. This

67 Chartres. The ox, the lion and the ram complementing the Green Men on the south transept portal in figure 68.

was to be followed in the later twelfth century by the sculptors of the nave of Notre-Dame de Paris where — for the first time since Roman imperial art but with a wholly different purpose — they began to portray definite and recognizable species of plants carved with delight and enjoyment as signs of the goodness of creation.

From this time onwards a new spirit entered Western art: that of exact observation of the visible world. It grew out of the great change in the psyche of Western peoples, described earlier, when they turned under the influence of Christianity away from the old participatory culture of the pagan world. It also grew from the immense technological advances made in the course of the eleventh and twelfth centuries. It was to be of the profoundest significance in the development of Western science, based as it is upon observation and classification. The Gothic sculptors became skilled in the accurate delineation of plant forms to a degree far beyond the standard of illustration in the botanical texts of the period.

68 *Chartres*. Three Green Men, (left to right: vine, acanthus, and oak) on the south transept portal.

85

69 Chartres. God creating Adam: one of the Creation series in the north portal.

This ability to depict the individuality of each plant had its counterpart in one of the greatest achievements of the Gothic masters: the new ability to portray the individuality of human beings. Precision in the carving of vegetation, precision in the carving of the human face: both of these were to revolutionize the forms of the Green Man over the next three to four hundred years. The sculptors transformed the two main elements, leaf and human head, of which the Green Man is the composite. Furthermore, just as they learned to signify an oak not just by the shape of its leaves and its acorns but by the habit of its growth, the pattern of its leaf mosaic and the angular curves of its twigs, so they learned to express, far beyond the repertoire of Romanesque sculptors, the range of human character and emotion in facial expression. They rediscovered the subtle part played by the muscles of the face in conveying feelings. Where Romanesque sculptors could convey the majesty and authority of Christ and His Saints on the one hand and the terrors and miseries of the damned on the other, they were not adept at expressing happiness. The human smile is a re-creation of Gothic art: there is a fragment from St-Denis (now in the Walters Museum, Baltimore)[2] showing a silenus-like head surrounded by vine leaves; his face is about to break into a smile. It may well be the first hint of a smile in a Green Man. Where the Green Men of the Romanesque do not express grim, angry or demoniacally ferocious emotions, they have the hieratic calm or disinterest noted earlier. From now onwards the Green Man could be shown to be happy.

Thus the two outermost heads of the South Portal Green Men can be said literally to be wreathed in smiles while the centre head has the upwards curl of the smile in his acanthus mask. All three faces are modelled on different human types while they share an expression of calm benignity. Blackened and grimy as they have been allowed to become, these heads have a forcefulness and beauty that command attention even among all the wonders of Chartres. Their forcefulness may derive from the thought that they represent three great traditions at Chartres: the oak being sacred to the druids who, according to old belief, held the site of the cathedral as one of their holiest places; the vine, which was the symbol of Bacchus and later became that of Christ: and the acanthus, which is the plant of the central head and which was sacred both in the classical and northern traditions as a symbol of rebirth. There is a further Celtic reference in the waters carved beneath them, to the tradition of heads that rose out of sacred wells and prophesied.

What is the relationship of these three heads to the three beast heads, the ox, the lion, and the ram, that complement them on the façade? Does the presence here of vegetation spirits and of three representatives of the animal world signify the transforming effect of the resurrected Christ which the South Portal celebrates in the works of creation? There are some further connexions that suggest themselves. The Green Man of the oak is the Green Man of the forest while the Green Man of the vine is the Green Man of agriculture. They can therefore be seen as the ancient division of mankind into pastoral nomads and tillers of the soil, the division between Esau and Jacob: this is paralleled by the ram for the way of the shepherd and the ox for the way of the farmer. But what of those occupying the central place of honour, the acanthus-leaf mask and the lion head? The acanthus signifies the plants that cross the boundaries of farm and wild land, the herbs that flavour, heal, or poison: it transcends the categories of its fellows just as the lion as king of the beasts and as a symbol of the sun and of Christ transcends the division of tame and feral. The two sets of heads can also be seen as symbolizing the works of time as they are affected and exalted by the Resurrection. They both signify aspects of time: there is an ancient tradition of the mysteries of Serapis in which the head of the god is shown above the heads of three beasts signifying time: the wolf of the past, the lion of the present, and the dog of the future. This symbol survived into Renaissance times.[3] Here only the lion is the same as in this traditional presentation but the pattern is the same. If the beasts therefore symbolize time in immediate experience, then the Green Men symbolize time in its recurrent seasonal round: the oak for spring, the vine for autumn, and the evergreen acanthus for winter and summer.

If these sculptures are symbols of the works of time, that would accord well with the overall symbolism mentioned earlier of the transepts making the line of time at right angles to the line of eternity. Both portals to the north and south transepts were carved and erected at the same time, c.1210. The line of history runs therefore from the story of Creation (69) told in the central vault of the North Portal, flanked on either side not only by the triplets of Green Men supporting the beast heads but also by other Green Men as the end-stops to the moulding of the arch, to the personages of the Old Testament who foretold Christ and the genealogy of the Virgin, across to the south side of the cathedral where we find the other Green Men already described, beaming in triumph at the fulfilment of time in the coming of Christ to the Last Judgment.

Where the Green Men of the South Portal smile, the six heads under the beast heads of the North Portal convey a different mood (71). They are the heads of fresh-faced young men growing out of rays of fig leaves, and they

70 *Chartres*. St John the Baptist on the north portal, photographed close to his day 24 June, the only time when the sun shines directly on him. Compare his expression with those of the Green Men in the figure below.

71 *Chartres*. One of the two sets of Green Man heads on the north transept portal. These are on either side of the Creation sculptures (see figure 69).

*72 Freiburg im Breisgau.
The Green Man on the
pendant on the north
choir door.*

*73 opposite. Freiburg im
Breisgau. The creation of
the world and the Fall,
on the north choir door,
c. 1340. Underneath the
pendant above the door
is the Green Man in
figure 72.*

share the expression of yearning for the coming of Christ that appears in
the faces of the column statues on either side of the doors such as John
the Baptist (70). They clearly derive from the new form of the Green Man
to be seen in the arches of the Royal Portal sixty years earlier in date, in
which the fruit of plant life is expressed as a human head.

The appearances of the Green Man at Chartres in his three major aspects,
as leaf mask, as disgorger of vegetation, and as the fruit of plant life, provide
us with some of the main contexts in which he was to flourish in the succeeding
generations of Gothic art and architecture, including themes of resurrection
and of the Last Judgement — and therefore with Christ — and with themes
that involve birth and the Incarnation — and therefore with the Virgin Mary.
Here it could be objected that I am reading too much into what, after all,
is only one small part of the overall wealth of iconographical detail and significance of the sculpture and glass of Chartres. I hope to justify my reading,
first by the wealth of examples in which the Green Man appears in *similar*
contexts to those at Chartres, and second by this thought. If the Green Man
at Chartres is only incidental to the whole work of sacred art represented
by the totality of the cathedral, so is every window, capital, column, vaulting
rib, portal and flying buttress. They all lead back to what is the central mystery
of Chartres: its creation as a collaborative work of art unparallelled in Western
civilization since ancient Greece, extraordinary for the unity of impression
and of atmosphere created there in a mere twenty-six years by its architects,
masons and workers in stained glass; and resulting from a shared magnani-
mity that would be unimaginable without the evidence of that greatness of
soul in the cathedral itself. If people so wise, so talented, so self-effacing
in the surrender not only of their personal wills but of all future fame should
have considered the Green Man to be a vital and important image, then
we should take that as a lead to follow even if we cannot find answers to
all the questions his appearance here evokes? Why, for example, did they
multiply his image here so much in addition to the prominence he was given
in the architectural scheme as a whole? Apart from the forty-odd heads in
the earlier Royal Portal, not only is he shown twelve times in the North
and South Portals but, so I am reliably informed,[4] he is carved in some twenty
other places where he cannot normally be seen, up among the flying buttresses
of the chevet and along the corridors and parapets that form the passages
of communication in the upper part of the cathedral. That is, I think, because
he was intimately linked to their experience and philosophy of creativity.

The masons and clerical patrons of Chartres gave their authority to the
representation of the Green Man in his new form. As the example of Moissac
(42) has already shown, and as may be seen at Angers and Le Puy (57),
it was already usual for him to be represented in the sculptures over doorways.
What is new about the Chartres Green Men of the North and South Portals
is the prominence given to them and the new feeling in their faces. In their
portrayals of the Green Man as a benign and beaming image, they expressed
a new attitude to Nature, one in which she is no longer the terrifying enemy
of human existence of so much Romanesque sculpture but the kindly
ally of man. Here, through the image of the Green Man, the moods of
Nature become humanized; and the attitudes of man and woman are reflected
back to them in the principle of awakening consciousness underlying all
creation.

The Triumph of the
Green Man in the
Gothic Period

From this period onwards he is to be found everywhere in wood and stone carvings. He appears far more rarely in ceramics and in stained glass and I have seen only one instance in metalwork — an enamelled buckle now in the Musée de Cluny.[5] It can be explained that most representations of him in tiles, windows, and smithy work would, in any case, have cracked, or been smashed or melted down, but there may be another reason — and that is that he is an emblem specially reserved to the crafts from whose members alone the master architects of the Gothic style were appointed. They rose to these heights only if they had undergone their training in carpentry or masonry. This is a point I will return to when we consider what the Green Man must have meant to the masons themselves; but before that we must look further at iconographical contexts in which he appears.

It was in the nature of the Gothic style to afford infinitely more opportunities for sculptural decoration than the Romanesque. Although we continue to find him in tympana as at St-Urbain in Troyes, in corbels and in modillions, he is now to be found in vaulting bosses as a result of the general introduction of ribbed vaulting; on towers and spires, as with the examples of Freiburg im Breisgau (6) and Vendôme (62); in the gables of chapels ringing the choirs or chevets of cathedrals such as Notre-Dame de Paris and Cologne; in the spandrels of arches as well as in the capitals of columns; in the high carvings of triforia, as at Wells; as end-stops to the moulding of the surrounds of arches and windows; in choirstalls and their surrounds; on pulpita and rood screens; on tomb sculpture; and in the carvings of cloisters. He also moves out into the secular world and is to be seen in palaces and castles such as the Archbishop of Canterbury's hall at Mayfield or in the royal lodgings at Angers. In many of the diverse settings in which he appears there are certain constants or recurrent doctrinal associations; there are also many unfathomable mysteries. The constants are these: first, associations with themes of creation, the natural world, and the laws of time and space; second, associations with the Virgin Mary and the Incarnation; and third, associations with Christ, especially with themes relating to the Passion, Resurrection and Second Coming.

For all these constants we can start from the portals of Chartres. The Green Men on the North Portal, as was mentioned above, flank the supremely beautiful carvings of the Creation of the world and the Fall. This association is taken up in the carvings depicting the same subject along the front of the *coro* in Toledo Cathedral, where underneath each panel the Green Man is carved in cusped triplets. Under the Creation series at Freiburg im Breisgau on the north door of the choir, a grinning Green Man stares down at you from the pendant over the door itself (72 and 73). The Chartres North Portal also shows the forerunners and foretellers of Christ, and this theme is taken up on a huge scale on the inner side of the western façade of Rheims, where the story of the Old Testament is told in fifty-two niches containing statues (75). Every niche is surrounded by panels and spandrels of vegetation — oak, ilex, hop, strawberry and ivy among them — and from two of the spandrels Green Men in the leaf-mask form look out on the works of time.[6] Villard de Honnecourt, the thirteenth-century architect whose sketchbook is the only one to survive from this period, drew Green Men in the leaf-mask form (78) and in one drawing, he showed how they could be constructed out of curving shapes resembling the Egyptian *crux ansata* (77).[7] It has been suggested that

74 *Bourges*. A Green Man on the southernmost portal of the west front of the cathedral.

*The Triumph of the
Green Man in the
Gothic Period*

75 *Rheims.* Old
Testament figures
surrounded by
vegetation from the
inner façade of the west
front, *c.* 1240.

in using this ancient symbol of eternity he was hinting at an association
between the Green Man and Cosmic Man — the principle of humanity that
lies hidden behind both the purposes and the appearances of creation. Thus,
in one of the visions of St Hildegard of Bingen, she saw God, the macrocosm
and the microcosm all in human form. The head of the macrocosm is immediately beneath that of God; his body is a series of concentric circles the outermost
of which is a wreath of fire and water whose union makes *viriditas*, the green
of manifested life. Man the microcosm stands naked against the central point
of earth.[8]

There is a similar association hinted at in the medieval portrayal of genealo-
gies or sequences of history in the form and symbolism of the tree. Humanity
falls by eating of the Tree of Knowledge of Good and Evil, but in the legends
of the Invention of the Cross that tree provides the wood for Christ's crucifixion and the redemption of humanity. From the loins of Jesse springs the
tree of Christ's genealogy. In the *Liber Floridus* of Lambert of St-Omer the
Tree of Good is shown as the Church and the Tree of Evil as Synagogue.[9]

91

76 *Rheims*. Green Men in the spandrels of the inner façade. *Kathleen Basford.*

77 Two Green Men drawn by Villard de Honnecourt, from the ms. in the Bibliothéque Nationale.

Some of the most influential examples of tree symbolism are to be found in the works of the prophet Joachim of Fiore, whose images not only inspired Dante but were to be a sore trial to the rulers of the Church because of their influence on millenary movements and reformers. Followers of Joachim, in the thirteenth century and later, saw change predicted in his division of time, as follows: the Age of the Father, from Creation up to the birth of Christ; the Age of the Son, from the coming of Christ to their own time; and the Age of the Holy Ghost when the need for the institutions of the Church would vanish. There is one representation of history as a tree which appears in many manuscripts, showing the Father in the roots of the tree. Two curving trunks with vegetation curling out of them rise up to make three circles. The first point at which they cross is filled with the head of Christ — like a Green Man. At the second crossing the Holy Ghost appears, and the uppermost circle is filled with a luxuriance of foliage that symbolizes the glories of that Age.[10]

The tree or plant therefore was a symbol of organic growth through time. Dante describes the origins of time in the *Primum Mobile* as a plant with its roots in the pot of that great sphere within which the lesser spheres revolve, its fruits and leaves hanging down through them.[11] Each individual tree and plant was also considered to possess its signature, the imprint of divine meaning from the day of its creation. The Gothic sculptors were therefore aware of these meanings which would contribute to their inspiration in their exact delineations of individual species. So to look for the signature in a plant was a spur to discovering and portraying its individuality. The signature could also be traced through the plant's use in medicine, magic or the kitchen, as well as its possible links with Old and New Testament stories and Christian and pagan legends.[12] Two great saints, Hildegard of Bingen and Albertus Magnus, wrote treatises on the virtues and symbolism of plants. These ideas infiltrated the awareness of patrons and sculptors to such an extent that when a great work such as the inner west façade of Rheims was planned, it was decided in advance what plant should be carved in association with which figure in order to enhance the symbolic meaning of the whole.

There was a particular art in drawing out the symbolic meanings in a subject or story. This was to look for the allegorical, the moral, and the anagogic or mystical meanings in biblical stories. According to Hugh of St-Victor the student of holy writ should read the stories of the Bible and let them form pictures in his mind.[13] He should contemplate these pictures and then allow the allegorical meaning to arise from these — which concerned the inner relationships and patterns of history in the context of its transformation through the coming of Christ. Thus Samson bearing away the gates of Gath was a prefiguring of Christ opening the gates of hell, and the tree in Eden was a prefiguring of the cross on Golgotha. From that he could progress to the moral level and then to the anagogic. For an example of how this kind of thinking affected the symbolism of plants we can turn to Adam of St-Victor, a monk of the same Premonstratensian abbey as Hugh of St-Victor. He wrote a poem about the hazel nut, saying that the hazel nut symbolized Christ: the green sheath was His flesh, the wood of the shell the Cross and the kernel His hidden divinity.[14] The hazel nut, even so, is a whole containing all these meanings — as a biblical story also contains many depths of significance. Thus when we find hazel leaves and nuts carved in corbels and bosses, as at Exeter, their presence there may allude to this interpretation. The same technique of interpretation was possibly applied to the Green Man.

The leaf carvings of the chapter house of Southwell Minster are generally regarded, with those of Rheims and Naumburg, as the supreme achievements of their kind in the thirteenth century. In all these examples the Green Man appears among the foliage. There are nine forms of him carved at Southwell with, in addition, an associated figure to which I will come later (81). Many different kinds of vegetation have been discerned in the leaves of Southwell, each with their signatures of the divine impress. The chapter house at Southwell was used not only for the internal business of the Minster canons but as a law court for the administration of justice within their lands and property. Medieval law was meant to be founded on Natural Law, the law with which God imbued creation from His Divine Law. We have already seen how, as early as the second century AD, in the early Christian writing *The Shepherd of Hermas*, the twigs of the cosmic tree were described as the Law of God, exemplifying the vital power implanted in the earth at His Incarnation (see p.46). In the development of the image, with the force of scholastic thought brought to bear on it, the essential goodness of Natural Law was seen to have existed since the first Creation. The laws of man, made necessary by the Fall, should nevertheless be based on the understanding of Natural Law. Can it be that the Green Man, peering out as he does from the gables of the stalls of Southwell (79), smiling from the vaulting bosses of the chapter houses at Noyon and Wells, and as part of the crowds of heads in the canopies of the chapter house at York, was in all these cases a personification of the intelligence underlying Natural Law and a reminder to those who regulated communities or administered justice to the common man and woman of the principles by which they should be guided?

The intelligence underlying the life of vegetation may be related to another line of thought and imagery. In the height of the Rheims inner façade God is shown as a haloed Christ figure issuing out of the Burning Bush to appear before Moses, who holds the tablets of the Law. It is a sublimely beautiful piece of carving: here the sculptor makes dramatic use of the theme of the Tree of Life, the tree of inspiration and prophecy, and causes it to erupt into the human figure of a God whose face is benign with love. This ensemble defines within the context of a story the principle I noted earlier of the tendency of vegetation to become humanized and to sprout human heads and bodies as its fruits or flowers. The most notable example given was of the forty-odd

78 Two leaf faces by Villard de Honnecourt, from the ms. in the Bibliothéque Nationale.

93

heads sprouting round the tympana of the Royal Portal of Chartres. It is developed later into the man who peers out of vegetation or rises with the whole or upper part of his body out of foliage. Thus is he shown in the crossing capitals at Laon. At Vendôme he rises out of a vaulting boss in one of the chapels of the chevet, smiling and pointing upwards in a mysterious but inviting way. At Southwell he looks out from the apex of the vine frieze that rises from the dragons at either side of the entrance portal to the chapter house (80 and 81). The vine is, of course, a symbol of Christ but this man, though his expression is one of calm happiness and of liberated feeling, bears no resemblance to any contemporary representations of Christ. These are only some of the examples of this figure we have found. One of the most unexpected is in the doorway inserted in the fifteenth century into the remarkable twelfth-century gabled porch of Clonfert cathedral in the west of Ireland. Here again he is associated with vine leaves. Who is this man? I think that he is either the Green Man unmasked or the Green Man who has disgorged his leaves and, having done his duty, is allowed to rise up and point to new wonders in life. If the leaves from which he rises have the special signature of their virtues imprinted in them, he bears the special signature of man, which is consciousness. He points to the celestial paradise where Dante, making his profession of faith, said:

> Le fronde onde s'infronda tutto l'orto
>   de l'ortolano etterno, am'io contanto
> quanto da lui a lor di bene e porto.[15]

> I love the leaves wherewith is all enleaved
>   The Eternal Gardener's garden, great and least,
> In the measure of the good from Him received.

It is through leaves and flowers also that we find the Green Man connected with the Virgin Mary. As her cult grew in influence during the twelfth and

80 *Southwell*. A mutilated dragon whose tail turns into the vine leaves round the outer frieze of the chapterhouse portal.

79 *opposite. Southwell.* One of the nine Green Men in the chapterhouse, *c.* 1290.

81 *Southwell*. The man appearing out of the vine leaves at the apex of the portal, *c.* 1290.

82 *Trier.* A cluster of three Green Men in the Liebfrauenkirche, *c.* 1240. *Kathleen Basford.*

84 *opposite. Norwich.* The Green Man as the face of inspiration: a famous example in the east cloister range carved 1415 by John Watlington with Brice the Dutchman.

83 *Ely.* One of the eight Green Men in the vaulting of the Lady Chapel, 1335–53.

thirteenth centuries, the portrayals of her changed from the solemn Black Virgins of the past to young and delightful girls. She too became associated with vegetation and especially with plants and flowers, as may be seen in the bas-reliefs on the plinths of the Chartres North Portal or in the leaf and flower carvings of Notre-Dame de Paris and of Rheims, or in the main tympanum of the Elisabethskirche at Marburg. Her blue mantle of the sky protected all the vegetation of the earth and the names of many plants were changed to reflect the service they offered her — as her bedstraw, her cushion, her lace, her slippers and her gloves. In this she became an exalted personification of Nature, idealized as the Queen of Heaven and identified with Wisdom as in the books of Solomon. She appears frequently identified with trees, as in Nicholas Froment's *Le Buisson ardent* in the cathedral of Aix-en-Provence or in the various representations of the Tree of Jesse as at Freiburg im Breisgau.

The association between the image of the Green Man as the disgorger of vegetation and the Virgin appears clearly in a story of a rich but illiterate knight who joined the Cistercian Order. The monks were ashamed of his lack of letters and tried to teach him to read and pray, but all he could remember was the words 'Ave Maria'. He died and was buried. Out of his grave there grew a lily with 'Ave Maria' in letters of gold on every petal. The monks, eager to know the source of the miracle, dug down into the grave and found that the lily grew out of the dead man's mouth. They then understood the depths of his devotion.[16] It is a story that has the same quality of simple happiness as the Green Man often radiates when in proximity to the Virgin in churches dedicated to her or in Lady Chapels. Thus, in one of the rare examples of him to be found in stained glass, he is to be seen as a smiling crowned foliate head beneath the Virgin in a window in St Mary Redcliffe, Bristol. In one of the most beautiful of all Gothic churches, Santa Maria del Mar in Barcelona, the bosses of the nave tell the life of the Virgin in progression towards the high altar which is ringed by great columns from whose capitals beam fourteen Green Men. In the Liebfrauenkirche (the Church of Our Lady) in Trier, built from 1235 onwards, three of the wings of the centrally planned space have a triplet of Green Man heads below the clerestory windows and the arrangement of the heads in threes seems to derive directly from those on the South Portal of Chartres (82).

He also appears prominently in the Lady Chapels of some of the English cathedrals, such as those of the vaulting bosses of the Lady Chapel of Ely Cathedral. The mutilated remains of canopies and niches ringing the chapel still preserve fine leaf carvings and two Green Man heads that were spared by Cromwell's soldiers. Fortunately they did not attack the vaulting, where eight Green Men look down at us (83), expressing a full range of moods, their faces framed by deep-cut vegetation. One watches from behind a cross formed of foliage, two others beam from trifoliate leaves with more leaves coming out of their mouths, another sprouts foliage from his ears as well as his mouth, a fifth has a huge protruding tongue, a sixth combines a demonic leaf mask with disgorging vegetation, a seventh with ecstatic joy radiates leaves like a sunburst, and an eighth in the leaf-mask form has a calm and happy expression. It is as though the sculptor intended to capture the special atmosphere or spirit of different weathers and seasons in the countryside and the essence of how Nature appears on particular days. Here in his attend-

ance on the Virgin he seems to become the poet of Our Lady, the man who knows the feminine side of his nature and can express the feelings of the heart. She too appears there out of foliage with her son (16).

The beautiful high bower of the Ely chapel with its radiant space, and the curious effect of these vital faces looking down on one's upbent gaze, especially prompt more questions about the association of the Green Man with the Virgin. We can see it as a natural effect of the transference of belief and ritual from one faith to another: as the Virgin replaced the Great Goddess in her older aspects and as the month of May, the time of flowers, became the month of Mary, so it would be easy to assimilate the May King into her service, and that may well have been the association that grew up in the minds of many. It seems too trivial and too homely an explanation for a work of such theological and artistic sophistication and complexity. If we turn, however, to the association of the image of the Green Man with time and the doctrine of the Incarnation as the moment when God enters the works of time, then we may see the Green Man as the source of time with its roots in the mystery of eternity, upended as in Dante's metaphor so that the leaves form the fabric of history. It was in this spirit, perhaps, that the clerics and canons permitted his portrayal in so holy and exalted a place and, as they let him appear, so unwittingly they were allowing the return of the ancient associations of the image.

One of the best places to see the close connexion of the Green Man with the Virgin is in Exeter Cathedral. There are some twenty examples of the Green Man inside the cathedral and they start in the Lady Chapel itself, the earliest part to be built in the rebuilding programme that began in 1275 and, continuing over the next eighty years, was to create one of the most unified interiors of all English great churches. Two Green Men sprouting artemisia or wormwood leaves, perhaps signifying the bitterness of the Passion, share one of the bosses of the ambulatory which bears leaf carving equal to that of Southwell in quality (87). The Green Man is also to be seen several times over in the high vaulting of the presbytery and choir, and it is in the two corbels of the choir itself that we see the link with the Virgin most particularly made. In one of these (47), often described as one of the most charming pieces of early fourteenth-century sculpture, the Virgin and Child stand on the head of a happy Green Man from whose mouth issues the foliage that creates a wood as background not only for the mother and child but also for two censing angels. The corbel next to it also rises from the head of a Green Man (86). Here an angel playing a viol stands on the head of the Green Man, who gives out oak foliage rising to contain the scene of the Coronation of the Virgin. At the west end of the nave there is a later corbel showing the same subject, this time rising from the Tree of Jesse (88). Next to it is a corbel with its vegetation rising out of the head of a young smiling king (18). He could well represent the May King or Summer Lord. So rich both in numbers of Green Men and of exuberant foliage is Exeter Cathedral that it arouses another thought. One of the symbolic meanings of the ground plan of a church was that it represented the body of a man with his legs forming the nave, his heart and arms the crossing and the transepts, and his head the choir. At Exeter one would be forgiven for thinking that the whole cathedral represents the Green Man in his totality and that the numerous representations of him are there to signal this meaning.

86 *Exeter*. A choir corbel showing an angel playing a viol supported by a Green Man with, above, the Coronation of the Virgin, before 1309. This corbel is next to that shown in figure 47 and was also probably carved by William Montacute.

85 *opposite*. *Dijon*. The Green Man as the disgorger of vegetation: a vaulting boss now in the Musée Archéologique, late thirteenth century.

97

The absorption into Christianity of these ancient associations through the image of the Green Man is equally clear where he is shown in the context of the Passion, the Resurrection and the Second Coming. The sequence of days of mourning and rejoicing for the death and resurrection of Attis were, as we have seen, taken over for the Easter rituals by the early Church. The large numbers of ritual deaths and resurrections recorded in the annals of folklore show how widespread the cult of the vegetation god was in much of Europe. These influences were quietly taken up in the portrayals of the Passion and Resurrection. The Green Man is often to be found carved on or close to rood screens, so called because they carried the rood or crucifix. Thus the Green Men at Llangwm (10) are carved in capitals just behind the rood screen and at South Molton (109) he is to be seen on capitals close to where the rood screen formerly stood. Tucked away in facing corners of the vaulting of the glorious Decorated pulpitum of Exeter Cathedral, where the organ now takes the place of the crucifix, are two Green Man heads. Again, in the west choir screen at Naumburg, the story of the Passion is told in a sequence of panels in the upper register. These in themselves are among the greatest and most moving examples of Gothic sculpture, and the wonderful leaf carvings supporting the Passion series remind us that life springs out of death and new faith out of dead creeds. Every leaf capital there was chosen for its significance for the story of the Passion[17] — and in the wall of the screen there is a most curious Green Man. His face is formed entirely of bark instead of leaves as if to signify that with the death of Christ he too has had to withdraw all signs of life into himself.

The connexion between him and the Passion is also to be seen in his appearances on Easter sepulchres, the tombs on which an image of the dead Christ was either placed in the Good Friday rites as at Lincoln, or else lay there permanently as in the example of Freiburg im Breisgau (21). It is as a symbol of rebirth and of Resurrection that we are most likely to find him from the thirteenth century onwards. He became a popular emblem to carve on tombs — on the shrines of saints such as those of St Frideswide in Oxford and of St Etienne d'Aubrazine, on the tombs of great nobles such as that of Edmund Crouchback in Westminster Abbey and of Louis de France, formerly in St-Denis, on the tomb of Bishop de Wich in Chichester cathedral and on the tombs of lesser worthies such as the sequence of gabled tombs in Winchelsea. In the case of the tomb of a priest, at Harpswell in Lincolnshire, the footrest of his body is an immense foliate mask[18]. One of the most intriguing examples of his appearances in funeral monuments is in a gabled tomb in the south ambulatory at Tewkesbury: here the Green Man's head appears at the centre of the gable. In one corner stands the figure of a just man, in the other a demon. The Green Man here is placed above right and wrong, above judgment and division. He is the energy of life that includes all.

The Resurrection of Christ is the promise of resurrection for all humanity at the end of time. We have seen the Green Man associated with Creation, with the organic growth of history, with the transformation of history through the Incarnation, and with the Passion. He continued to appear frequently whenever the Second Coming was portrayed, as at Bourges and as in the many examples I have already given. The west front of Poitiers with its central tympanum of the Last Judgement provides a particularly fine example. Not only are there six huge leaf masks of the Green Man placed at the angles

88 *Exeter*. A corbel carving from the nave showing the Virgin and Child supported by Jesse with the tree growing from his loins and, above, the Coronation of the Virgin, *c*. 1350.

87 *opposite. Exeter*. Two Green Men sprouting artemisia or wormwood leaves on a single boss in the cathedral ambulatory, late thirteenth century.

99

89 *Lincoln*. The head of Christ censed by angels growing out of vegetation, in the south choir transept, thirteenth century.

of the arcade of niches that lead in to the three doors, but up above are Green Man heads glowing with pleasure at the final redemption of time.

In associating him with time in the sense of linear Christian history stretching from the first Creation to the Last Judgement I have been employing the allegorical level of interpretation. Allegorical interpretation concerns what we believe and what we are told about the events of time in Christian doctrine. If we look at the Green Man and his associated foliage in the light of the moral level of interpretation, we learn from him about what we should do.

If there is a single message that we receive from Gothic art, it is that we should give praise. And that is what we should do with the time God has given us. In the case of the Green Man his ancient Celtic role as the head that prophesies, that sings and utters verses, returns in a new setting. If the suggestion is correct that he can be seen as uttering the Logos as foliage, then he acquires a cosmic dimension on this level as well.

It was one of the great gifts of the Gothic Masters to reveal creation to us not as a world of temptation and lust but as the starting point for praise of the Creator. Leaves and tendrils, which had been the images of temptation

90 *Marburg*. One of the many Green Men on the *Lettner* or pulpitum of the Elisabethskùrche. See also fig. 48.

100

and Fall, were transformed into the expression of God's love for the world. 'By their fruits shall ye know them' became a text for a positive turning to God and an incitement to acts of praise, instead of an injunction to condemn. The leaf and fruit became symbols of the good deeds and words of men. Among these good deeds and words are the reading of the Gospel, the preaching of the truth and the singing of songs of praise. If we needed further proof of how far the Celtic tradition of the severed head that sings and utters truths and prophesies had been assimilated into the Gothic tradition, we have only to turn to the pulpitum or *Lettner* at Marburg, which is crowded with Green Men out of whose mouths pour the leaves of good tidings (48 and 90). From this pulpitum the Gospel was sung during celebrations of the Mass. Choirs and choirstalls were also particularly favoured places for the Green Man: what pours out of him as vegetation freely given to the Lord should pour from the monks and choristers in psalms and anthems. So we find the Green Man frequently carved both on the misericords

91 *Winchester*. A Green Man armed with sword and buckler in the cathedral choirstalls carved 1308 by William Lyngwode.

92 *Norwich*. A Green Man in the south cloister range of the cathedral, early fourteenth century.

93 *opposite. Poitiers*. A Green Man radiating like a sunburst in the thirteenth century cathedral choirstalls.

which supported the singers during the offices and sung masses, and also on the sedilia backs and in the canopies above their heads as at Poitiers, and in the choirstalls carved by William Lyngwode at Winchester in 1308 (91). At Tewkesbury there is a magnificent series of Green Men in the vaults of the transepts on either side of the place where the monks sang. If he is associated with praise, he is also to be found in places of silence, contemplation and study such as cloisters. Some of the most radiant carvings of him are to be seen in the cloisters at Norwich (84 and 92). There are at least ten examples of him in the cloisters of Trier Cathedral.

The cathedral at Poitiers preserves one of the most complete and mysterious ensembles of Gothic sculpture to have survived. The form of the Green Man as a leaf mask radiating like a sunburst which appears on the west front is reproduced in the same form as a spandrel carving of the choirstalls, which are also thirteenth-century and are said to be the earliest of their kind in France. He is placed here (93) among forty other spandrel carvings which survive from many more which have been lost. They are both extremely beautiful and utterly baffling. Each subject is alternated with the repeated theme of an angel rising out of water and offering two crowns. Are they the crowns of the active and the contemplative lives or do they signify something more arcane? Though many of the subjects are capable of individual interpretation on the moral level because they are familiar from carvings in other churches, such as the man who falls from his horse, signifying pride, we find the Green Man here among a series of carvings which are sometimes linked with him in theme – such as the smiling man who feeds a dragon whose claws turn into luxuriant oak leaves and acorns. In another spandrel

a bearded fool sprouts arum leaves from his hood. There are animals such
as the basilisk, the amphisbaena, dragons, lions, a centaur, a griffin, the phoenix, a cat eating a rat, a bat and a cockerel. One of the finest of all the carvings
is that of an architect, smiling as he traces a design with his compasses,
supported by his plumbline and his square. The only attempt I know of to
interpret the whole ensemble is an alchemical one in which the Green Man
here is said to be the symbol of sulphur or the philosopher's sun of the
Great Work.[19] This interpretation gives another view to my own feelings
on examining these carvings. These were as though I were faced with a wonderful mystical poem with many levels of meaning, with images that on one
level could represent wickedness and on another were stages in a series of
trials and testings, of transformations and strange meetings on a journey
that would end in the purification of the soul. It is not only the Green Man
and the architect who are smiling here: every angel and nearly every human
face is depicted with an expression of pleasure, even the miser.

What are they smiling at? The pleasure of the architect in his craft gives one indication. He is making the time given to him fruitful; he knows what his direction is; he is the master of his craft. Such a thought leads us to the possible interpretation on the highest level of all, the anagogic. This level is concerned with the mystical way in this life and our goal in the next life. In both senses it is the level of unity desired or attained with the divine. If, as St James says, 'every good gift and every perfect gift is from above', it is also the level of the highest and most profound inspiration.

The reason why the Green Man is to be found wherever the Gothic masters worked is that he was to them the symbol of the most precious gift they could receive from above, the gift of inspiration. Through their years of training and apprenticeship they could acquire through their efforts every skill possible: to manifest that skill two things were necessary that were beyond their control. One was the opportunities for great commissions; the other was the descent of the inspiration that would make them equal to the commissions when they came. For both of these, like the wise virgins they so often carved in their churches, they had to keep the lamps of the spirit trimmed.

If we were to sum up what the greatest achievement of the Gothic masters was, we could say that it was a new conception of man in relation to the universal and to Nature. They expressed this in three main ways: the first and grandest is the incarnation of divine light into Gothic space; they recreated the holy glades and avenues of forests in stone and in doing so they gave us new insights to the immensity of the human mind in contemplation of the divine unity and of the works of creation. They made space sing a new song. Inside and outside their new spatial arrangements they carved fresh interpretations of the works of time — men, women, beasts and plants. The second of their achievements was the presentation of man and woman as individuals whose experience and character is expressed through their features, clothes and movements within the context both of history and of eternity. In this they gave new meaning to the Christian conception of the individual nature of the human soul. Their third achievement was in realizing the individuality of the species of life, most especially plant species.

The Green Man can be seen to encapsulate all these achievements. As cosmic man or the personification of the intelligence in the tree of life, the Green Man is the point at which truth is manifested in creation, whether as life, light, song, words or the figurative forms of art. He is the medium through which divine inspiration guides the works of time in the fullness of space. He is the point of entry of eternity into time. Space is the medium of sound and therefore of the music of praise. The masons and their fellow workers practised an art of praise in this way aspiring to an angelic art as may be seen at Vendôme (95) or in the depiction of the angels censing the head of Christ as it appears out of foliage at Lincoln (89). This last carving seems to signify the renewal of the energies of life brought about by Christ and to echo St Hildegard's statement that Christ was the green wood because He bore the greenness of the virtues.[20]

The second and third achievements of the Gothic masters may also be seen in him in this way: he combines the human head, portrayed with all the individuality his carvers gave to the characters from biblical stories and from the lives of the saints, with the foliage the carvers also studied so keenly and represented with such depth of emotion.

95 *Vendôme*. A mason bows to measure with his compasses guarded by an angel rising out of foliage in the capital above: from the transepts of St Trinité.

105

The Triumph of the
Green Man in the
Gothic Period

If the Green Man is often seen to grimace or suffer as well as smile, in his suffering he represents the sacrifice of the masons in surrendering their personal hopes and ambitions to the greater inspiration that came to them through the tradition of which they were part.

How important a part of that tradition the image remained may be seen in the work of one of the last great architects in the style, Jean Texier de Beauce. When he was rebuilding the west front of the Abbey of the Trinity at Vendôme, he had to place his work beside the twelfth-century spired tower with the Green Men in its angle buttresses. Amid the florid tracery of his façade he made sure that once again the Green Man was given his place of honour over the portals. In 1506 the wooden spire of the north-west tower of Chartres was burnt: Jean Texier was commissioned to replace it with a lantern and spire of stone, which he carried out between 1507 and 1513. Furthermore, he had to produce a work of art that would complement and not disgrace the south-west tower or *vieil clocher*, which is one of the supreme achievements of the early Gothic period. It was the spire of this tower that set the model for the steepled landscapes of Europe. It was also this tower that first expressed the anagogic meaning of the spire in Gothic art: it points us to our ultimate goal in heaven. From this spire followed all the miraculous creations such as Salisbury, Strasbourg, and the spire of Freiburg im Breisgau which first set me on my hunt for the Green Man. Jean Texier employed the same principles of proportion in constructing his tower as those used on the south-west tower,[21] even though he was to use the architectural language of his time. That architectural language now included the influence from Italy of Renaissance styles, so that the lantern from which the spire ascends is in fact a Renaissance octagonal pavilion with classical pilasters and capitals, largely masked from below by the flamboyant decoration of the parapet and the arches at the angles. On the capitals of one of the angles of the lantern you will find the Green Man in his classical form ready to play his part in a new age of invention and discovery.

Chapter 6

Masterpieces and Mysteries

If it is correct to see in the Green Man a symbol of creativity then, simply because of that association, the image will be richer in meanings than any analysis or method of exploration can be expected to uncover. An archetype when expressed through great art not only reveals many layers of meanings: it also faces us with far more mysteries than we would ever have suspected. Here I will take six examples of portrayals of him, some single, some in ensembles. All are masterpieces and all are mysterious. Although in the last chapter I was concerned to show how completely he had been accepted into Western Christian iconography, several of the examples that follow will demonstrate how far he could keep the meanings of the pagan past.

My first example concerns the heads in the ambulatory of Auxerre Cathedral. The choir and ambulatory were begun in 1215. All round the ambulatory just above head height there juts out a series of massive heads. The size of these heads is characteristic of Burgundian Gothic: similar heads are to be seen for example at St-Thibault and Semur-en-Auxois. It is, perhaps, one of many instances of the strong influence of the Gallo-Roman remains in Burgundy on the Romanesque and Gothic art of the region: in this case, the influence of the Celtic veneration of the human head.

This series of heads depicts the prophets of the Old Testament, the sibyls of classical antiquity, and Green Men (98, 97, 96, 99 and 100). We know why the prophets are there: because they foretold the coming of Christ. We know why the sibyls are there: on the basis of late classical writings attributed to their oracles they also were thought to have foretold the coming of Christ. The writings were later revealed as forgeries but the message they conveyed was too impressive for their authenticity to be questioned. Why then does the Green Man appear here in several distinct forms? One shows him as a crowned king with sweeping moustaches of foliage (96); others are leaf masks with stern, authoritative faces (99 and 100). They are presented here as equal in merit with the prophets and priestesses of the past and, presumably, as tellers of the same message as their companions. We know that to the Celts the human head possessed the properties of prophecy and divination. We know of Irish legends that say that the druids were aware of the events and significance of the Crucifixion at the time it occurred.[1] Can some similar story surviving in Burgundy account for the presence of the Green Men in this sequence?

Auxerre Cathedral is built on the site of a Gallo-Roman temple. A well authenticated story tells of an annual rite that was performed every Easter on the labyrinth that was formerly set in the floor of the nave.[2] Here the dean and the canons would gather in a circle and while they danced and sang they would throw a large golden ball from one to another. This has

98 *Auxerre*. One of the Old Testament Prophets in the ambulatory.

97 *Auxerre*. A sibyl who prophesied the coming of Christ in the ambulatory.

96 *Auxerre*. A crowned Green Man with foliate moustaches: one of the series of heads in the cathedral ambulatory, after 1215.

100 *Auxerre*. A Green Man vibrant with the spirit of prophecy.

99 *opposite. Auxerre*. A fine-leaf mask Green Man, one of those who accompany the prophets and sibyls as foretellers of Christ.

been linked to the widespread Celtic legend that the sun on rising on Easter Day dances for joy at the Resurrection of Christ.

Whatever the reasons for his incorporation here among the foretellers of Christ, he is again seen in the context of history and of time — the time before Christ. He may, of course, represent the longing of all Nature for the redemption of the world — in which case he is the cosmic man or intelligence underlying creation. In order to long for something, you have to know or at least to hope that the object of your longing will come into existence. Through your longing for that consummation, you prophesy.

There is another point to note about the Auxerre Green Men: the prophets and sibyls, often have names carved in the stone above their heads. No names are given to the Green Men. Is this because everyone knew that he was *le feuillu* and there was no need to go to the bother of saying so? Or is it for some other reason? There is only one known instance where the Green Man has a name ascribed to him. This is on a fountain now in the Musée Lapidaire of St-Denis where beside an oak-leaf mask of the Green Man is carved the name Silvanus, that of the Roman god of the woods (101).[3] Silvanus was never portrayed with the characteristics of the Green Man in classical

111

101 *St Denis*. The only Green Man named on a carving: an oakleaf head on a fountain with 'Silvanus' inscribed above it, *c.* 1200. *Kathleen Basford*.

times. Vincent of Beauvais simply describes Silvanus as a god of the country-side and so gives little help. Villard de Honnecourt writes the name *teste de fuelles* besides his drawings.[4] Given the ubiquity of the image and the obvious importance of it, not to mention the love the Green Man attracted from his sculptors, it is extraordinary that these are the only indications — apart from the evidence of folklore gathered centuries later — of what he was called.

My next example is also from Burgundy and he harks back as much to Dionysos and the classical past as to Celtic origins (85 and 102). I came across him in a window embrasure of the Musée Archaeologique in Dijon and he is one of our favourites of all those we have seen. He is carved on a roof boss from the thirteenth-century Chapelle de Bauffremont, which was part of the Abbey of St-Bénigne and which was destroyed at the French Revolution. Fortunately he retains his original paint. The branches of vine leaves that come out of his mouth are in their autumnal colours, offsetting the grapes he also offers. The vine brings with it the ancient associations of Dionysos and the mystery religions, and also the ways in which Christ spoke of Himself as the vine and in which early Christianity took over the Dionysiac symbolism. More than that, to me, this Green Man is the perfect exemplar of the marriage between the individualism of Gothic portraiture and the skill in the accurate portrayal of foliage in depictions of the Green Man which grows out of those on the south portal of Chartres. The fortunate survival of the paint enable us to realize the extra dimension of humanity that is revealed in the painting of the eyes. The Auxerre Green Men, for example, have their eyeballs pared at the place where their irises would have been painted but, alas, they were scrubbed and cleaned long ago. There is a marvellous intelligence in the eyes of this Dijon Green Man and there is a sense of modernity about this face that makes one feel one is in the presence of a real individual man — moreover, not a man of the thirteenth century but one who could be alive and conversing at any time from that period onwards. He could be someone whose friendship we would be proud to gain — not simply on the personal level of a man with a magnetic intelligence, but because his face expresses a range of qualities we have been led to admire by the tradition in which his carver worked: he observes, he questions, he discriminates, he founds his judgements in his own experience; and yet also he gives. The fruit of his experience is the vine, very suitably for a Burgundian Green Man, with all its associations of sacrifice, transformation and reward. There are many other representations in Burgundy of the Green Man giving out vines and grapes — two notable examples appear on the same capital at Semur-en-Auxois, a church which is a paradise for seekers after mystagogical interpretations — but there is a quality in this man, both in the art with which he is carved and the depth of emotion in his expression, which leaves me wondering how and why the sculptor chose this ancient image to be the vehicle of the line of understanding that was to influence so deeply the future of Western civilization.

Though you might hope to have the Dijon Green Man as your friend, it is unlikely that you would feel the same about my next example, the Green

102 *Dijon*. The Green Man from the Chapelle de Bauffremont. A side view of the head is shown in figure 85.

Man of Bamberg (103). The most you could hope for in any dealings with him is that he should be on your side. He is an acanthus-leaf mask acting as a corbel to the foliated ledge on which stands the famous Rider of Bamberg (104). Both Rider and Green Man have defied both individual identification and the narrative connexion in which they are joined. German scholars have identified the Rider variously as a King of Bohemia and as the Holy Roman Emperor ruling at the time of his carving (1235-9), Frederick II Hohenstaufen.[5] To the French historian Georges Duby he suggests St Louis.[6] There are more general indications of what the Rider signifies: just as on the moral level the rider falling from his horse signifies pride, so the rider who is in control of his horse is the master of his nature; in him head, heart and hand work in harmony. On an allegorical level he stands for just government — similar statues were erected in great German cities such as that at Magdeburg,[7] formerly opposite the Rathaus. In this case, to take up a theme from the last chapter, the Green Man is not, in what would be too easy and literal an interpretation, the pagan world over which the Christian Knight rides, but he is Natural Law which should guide and support human government. The ferocity of his expression is one of warning against neglect of Natural Law. Returning to the moral or psychological level in which the Rider is the man in control of his nature, the Green Man here warns against the crushing of natural instincts in an unbalanced attempt to maintain control. On the anagogic level, that of the journey of the soul to God, we find the meanings that seem best to suit the mood of the work as a whole: the questing spirit of the Rider, the watching eyes of the Green Man. The canopy above the Rider's head shows the towers of an ideal city that may be at once the earthly city under just government, the city of the righteous soul, and the heavenly Jerusalem.

It suggests to me as well another association. Elsewhere I have offered the thought that there is a strong Arthurian influence on this work.[8] Close to the time it was carved German poets were creating masterpieces of vernacular literature based on Arthurian stories: Gottfried von Strassburg was writing his *Tristan* and Wolfram von Eschenbach was dictating his *Parzival*. The crowned Rider might be a Grail Knight seeking the castle of Munsalvaesche. What then is the Green Man in this context?

My only approach to an answer is to take a flight into the next century and to North-West England, where a nameless poet wrote another Arthurian masterpiece: *Sir Gawaine and the Green Knight*. This is the only literary work of the Middle Ages in which a figure with something of the name and with many of the ancient and Christian characteristics of the Gothic Green Man appears. Though this is the only appearance of the Green Man in medieval literature, it is a resounding and memorable entry. I paraphrased the beginning of the story in the Prelude (pp.3–4), telling how a huge green man riding a green horse issues a challenge to Arthur's court. It is that he will submit to having his head struck from his shoulders if the knight who decapitates him will come to submit to a similar trial in a year's time. Gawaine accepts the challenge: the Knight dismounts and is decapitated. His body rises and picks up his head which speaks — like the head of St Melor — reminding Gawaine of his promise. When the autumn passes Sir Gawaine sets out to find the Green Knight. After many adventures he reaches a castle where he is entertained by the Lord, Sir Bertilak, and his lady. Sir Bertilak

103 *opposite. Bamberg.* The Green Man.

makes a bargain with Gawaine: when he returns from hunting he will present
Gawaine with the spoils of the day and Gawaine must equally present him
with what he has gained in the course of the day. While Bertilak hunts,
the Lady comes to Gawaine's bedside and entertains and tempts him with
talk of love. On the first day they exchange a kiss and when Sir Bertilak
returns, to fulfil his part of the bargain, Gawaine kisses him. On the second
day of conversation the Lady kisses Gawaine twice and Gawaine kisses Bertilak twice on his return. On the third day the Lady offers Gawaine a green
girdle entwined with gold which has the virtue of protecting the wearer from
any harm or blow. She also kisses him three times. On Sir Bertilak's return
Gawaine gives him the three kisses but withholds the girdle. Gawaine wears
this girdle secretly when he goes to his tryst with the Green Knight whom
he recognizes as Sir Bertilak. He submits to the trial by the axe. Twice the
axe is deflected and the third time the Green Knight wounds him in the
neck. Then he reveals to Gawaine that he knows about the gift of the girdle
and he chides Gawaine for his lack of honour. The drama has been set in
motion by the old lady who lives in the castle, Arthur's half-sister Morgan
le Fay. Gawaine then returns to Arthur's court a humbled man.

Sir Gawaine is full of elements from the past we have already seen, whether
in legend or works of art: death by decapitation, the speaking head, the
god who needs a human hero to assist him, and sacrifice. There are many
Celtic influences on the poem, one being the story of the *bachlach*, the wild
man who appears in *Briciu's Feast* (see p.30). Bertilak may be an Anglo-Norman
form of *bachlach*. Morgan le Fay comes from the Irish Great Goddess, the
Morrigan, and so the archetypal link between Goddess and Green Man is
maintained here. But just as the masons gave the image of Green Man new
power by bringing him into Christian contexts, so the poet sets this ancient
figure in the moral code of Christian chivalry giving him a fresh significance.
There were in fact two soldiers known as the Green Squire in the fourteenth
century.[9] Sir Bertilak in the poem is greater in character, strength and spirit
than any knight of Arthur's court. He is utterly courageous, utterly faithful
to his word, and utterly courteous. He trusts to death for his rebirth. He
lives as the grandest of princes, surrounded by all the evidence of wealth,
in the wildest and most inaccessible place. The three hunts, described with
vigour and detail, show him to be the lord of the forests. What would he
have done if Gawaine had kept his word and surrendered the girdle the
third evening? Would Sir Bertilak have revealed himself as the Green Knight
then and spared Gawaine the ordeal because, by handing over the girdle,
he had already acknowledged he was ready to meet his death? Or would
he have still enforced the terms and struck off Gawaine's head? And would
he then as lord of life and death have restored Gawaine to life?

As the girdle is green entwined with gold, so these colours are associated
throughout the poem, green standing for the resurgent energies of life and
gold for the values of civilization. The theme of green and gold also appears
in the earlier Arthurian poem, Wolfram's *Parzival*. To Wolfram the Grail is
not a chalice but an emerald on which messages appear in a script of gold.

Returning to the Green Man of Bamberg, let us look at what the sculptor
made of him. His leaf mask is formed of one acanthus frond, swelling out
from the brows to give the impression of massive intellectual power, made
all the more effective by the deep furrow of thought that cleaves his forehead.

104 *opposite. Bamberg.*
The Rider of Bamberg *c.*
1239. The Green Man is
on a console supporting
the ledge on which the
Rider stands.

The lobes of the frond make a beard, moustaches, cheekbones, forehead and hair. The lips and mouth, the nose and nostrils, the eyes with their heavy folds and deep-drilled pupils directed to his right are finely modelled, rising naturally out of the leaf forms to create a face that is of an individual, powerful, accustomed to rule, all-knowing and all-seeing. His command of everything that goes on in his domain is reinforced by the manner in which the holes formed by the overlapping of the leaf lobes seem to make a series of eyes through which he observes the world.

I know of no sculpture which is at once so frightening and so beautiful. No Gothic sculpture of the Devil and his demons, not even those at Bourges, can approach him for the impression of terror he conveys — and even less for the wholly satisfying aesthetic pleasure we can gain by contemplating him. He was made to shock: you approach him and the Rider above him along an ambulatory set with sculptures of the highest quality reflecting the influence both of Rheims and of deep study of classical sculpture. You see Mary and Elizabeth at the Visitation, you see an angel greeting the martyred St Denis, and between these groups you see older carvings of prophets in conversation with evangelists. Then you turn the corner and find the Green Man looking sideways straight at you.

If the other statues owe most to classical art and to Rheims, this Green Man has chiefly in his antecedents both the Roman examples of foliate heads like those on the Neumagen tombs (33) and the acanthus-leaf mask of the Green Man on the south portal of Chartres (68). Whereas the Chartres Green Man is benign and noble, the sculptor of Bamberg created in his own master-piece a wholly different atmosphere. He must have loved and enjoyed the image. He must have at the same time been profoundly aware of the dangers and powers within the image — memories of the ancient Teutonic worship of trees, of Wotan, the god of forests and of inspiration, of the capacity for wild and brutal cruelty in the tribal soul of his ancestors, as well as the Christian and classical associations with which he would have been consciously even more familiar. His preparation for carving it must have been like a journey towards his own death during which he had to face up to every fear and every malevolent impulse in his own soul until, as a gift or in moment of self-surrender, he was shown how face and acanthus frond could be united into a nodding fountain of foliage, rising and falling back on itself in a rhythm that married intensity of feeling to the habit of plant growth. Then, in the act of carving, true to the unitive vision within him, he created a representation of the archetype, so penetrating, so all-encompassing in its range of feelings, that it offers to the beholder the innumerable meanings that are the riches of great art.

Our next notable Green Man (105 and 106), carved some sixty-odd years later, would be considered a remarkable work of art if it were placed in one of the greatest of our cathedrals. It is all the more surprising to find him in the parish church of the small Wiltshire village of Sutton Benger, where he is much loved and admired. He is thought to be late thirteenth or early fourteenth century in date:[10] the sculptor also carved two small foliage corbels in the same style. There are medieval and Victorian Green Men also on the exterior of the church (2) and it has been suggested that this Green Man was subjected to recutting in the last century. It is hard to see how this could have been done except to the eyes, and here the deep cutting is parallelled

105 *opposite. Sutton Benger*. The Green Man inside the parish church *c*. 1300. A Green Man on the outside of the church is shown in the frontispiece.

119

by other medieval examples such as the Bamberg Green Man; no repairs have been carried out to the damaged parts of the foliage and the face. It is probably the modernity and the individualism of the face that have prompted this suggestion but those are both characteristic of other Green Men we have considered, such as the Green Man in the Musée Archéologique at Dijon — and it is hard to think of a sculptor working in England in the 1850s, the time of the restoration of Sutton Benger church, capable of such expressiveness as is shown in this Green Man.

The Sutton Benger Green Man is placed at the western end of the south aisle of the church. It is hard to guess whether he formed part of a wider grouping, though it is tempting to think that he was once accompanied by a statue or painting of the Virgin and Child, as in the iconographic connexion we have seen at Exeter and Ely, for example. Out of his mouth pour the twisting twigs of hawthorn rising in a swirling rhythm of undulating leaves between which hang bunches of haws. Four birds perching on the outsize leaves peck at the haws. The vigour of the foliage indicates spring: the presence of the berries indicates autumn. It is as though the range of the seasons are present and known to him. As for his face, it is of a power to make you draw back and compose yourself: not because it is daunting like the Bamberg face, but because, in other ways like the Bamberg face, of the range of experience and emotions it expresses. It is the face of a monk in a cowl of hawthorn leaves, ascetic, shallow-cheeked with the effort of giving forth. Under his thick and curling eyebrows, his eyelids are deep-set under the frontal bone: the pupils and the lachrymal ducts are deep-drilled and the folds beneath the eyes drop away as though they were the shadow marks of one who, like Dante, had thought 'the things that are hard to think'.[11]

It is as one examines him from different angles that one starts to grasp something of the complexity of emotions he expresses. Seen in profile, he is all sacrifice: he is like one of the bog people such as Tollund Man, a willing victim for the good of the community. When seen from above, he conveys a melancholic resignation. Seen from below with the foliage and the birds rising like a garlanded bower above him, he has the look of a man who is happy in being centred in an act of perpetual praise. When you look straight at his eyes, you are met by a gaze full of wisdom and patience. The sculptor has caught the natural asymmetry in shape and expression of eyes in the human face so that they convey the complexity of exchange between the outward and the inward nature of man. The differences between the eyes mirror the creative tension out of which the sculptor has carved him: it is the same as the contrast between the exuberance of the foliage and the asceticism of the face.

The hawthorn that comes out of his mouth could be thought at first to arouse the associations of the May King and the many mentions of the tree in medieval lyrics and literature. From the Church's point of view the hawthorn had a bad name: it was the *arbor cupiditatis*, the tree of desire.[12] The yeasty scent of its blossom arouses sexual desire: its boughs were cut down at night on the eve of May when young men and women went off to the woods to sing and make love and to return on May morning with the maypole round which they danced, in the presence of the May King and the Queen of the May. It was one of the least repressible survivals of the old religion. Yet when we look at this Green Man we find no riotous young leader of

106 *Sutton Benger*. The full face view of the Green Man.

revels, but a man of experience and restraint; equally it is hard to see any condemnation of the hawthorn's known associations in the way its foliage is depicted here.

This is one of the puzzles about the Green Man in many of his finest representations in the Gothic period: the greater the sophistication of his carving and the deeper the sense of individuality given to his face, the less he seems to have to do with folk custom or survivals of pagan ritual in the merely superstitious sense. Their mood and intention indicate a different level of meaning and intention. The very modernity of the faces points not to the past but to the present and the future, through the new understanding of the relationship between man and Nature brought about by the architects and sculptors of the Gothic style. To say this is not to deny the presence of ancient influences in them: it was through striving so hard to reach the archetype underlying the Green Man that the sculptors found these influences

121

107 Crediton. A Green
Man with foliage issuing
from his eyes as well as
his mouth.

rising up so strongly in their works.

Ordinary people may well have seen in him the leaf-covered figures of
their seasonal festivals and enjoyed his presence in their churches as a result
of his associations. Many of his representations in country churches such
as those of Devon have been interpreted as grotesque, diabolic, and frightening — and not only in country churches. Mrs Basford says that the 'association
between the human and plant elements is often suggested as an uneasy or
actually hostile relationship rather than a balanced symbiosis. Sometimes the
leaves appear parasitic, drawing their strength from the wretched head which
bears them.'[13] She points to a hideous Green Man from Melrose Abbey in
which bloated leaf stalks appear in the eyes and the mouth, and to another
at Ottery St Mary where the stalks grow out of the pupils of the eyes.

I do not take the example at Ottery St Mary or a similar head at Crediton
(107) in the same way that she does. If the Green Man is a symbol of inspiration, then the leaves coming out of the eyes indicate the artist entering
so fully into the world before him that he becomes what he sees or makes.
On the chancel arch at South Molton, another church with many examples
of the image, beside a Dionysos-like Green man there is a carving of a man
with a strong, curious and questing expression. He is said locally to be the
mason of the church: there is a detail in the carving which would support
this identification. The fingers of his right hand, folded under his left hand,
have turned into fronds of vegetation. His fingers have become themselves
like the foliage and Green Men they had carved on the capitals of the church
(108 and 109).

South Molton is one of the many Devon churches close to the recently
discovered Woodhenge (see p.53). The affection for the image in the town

108 *South Molton*. A carving on the chancel pier said to represent the fifteenth century mason of the church. The fingers of his right hand turn into foliage.

109 *South Molton*. On the capital to the right of the mason (above) a Dionysiac Green Man gives out grapes and vine leaves.

lasted long after the fifteenth-century rebuilding of the church, for there are fine Green Men to be seen in the town hall of 1743 and on a nineteenth-century row of shops in the Ruskinian Gothic style. There is a strong presumption that the image appeared in such places because of attachment to ancient beliefs and superstitions. But there is another reason for his appearance in the churches of this area. The Green Man is not only a symbol of prosperity: he is evidence of prosperity. The large number of churches rebuilt throughout Cornwall, Devon and Somerset in the fifteenth and sixteenth centuries, and richly furnished with carvings that so often included the Green Man, are a sign of the prosperity of these counties at the time. If you could afford carving you could afford Green Men, because they were part of the repertoire of images the craftsman had to offer you. In contrast, the part of Sussex I am most familiar with has few Green Men because it was a poor, wildly wooded region for much of the Middle Ages. There is little carving to be found because hardly anyone could afford it. It was the last outpost of paganism in Southern England. It was also an area rich in folklore and legend of the very kind that one would expect to find mirrored in representations of the Green Man. It had dragons, it still keeps many remembrances of the Great Goddess, its villagers probably performed the spring and harvest rites of birth, death and renewal; but there is no counterpart of this surviving in the churches.

A prodigal expenditure of wealth accounts for our next examples of the Green Man in Roslin chapel, south of Edinburgh, built in the 1450s by the last of the Sinclair Princes of Orkney. The chapel contains the most richly decorated interior to have survived from what was one of the greatest periods in Scottish cultural history. Only the choir and part of the transepts were built, and it must be said that the encrustations of carvings were in many cases subjected to savage cleaning and retooling in the last century.[14]

The chapel consists of a high aisle whose tunnel vault is carved with flowers and rosettes. The retro-choir, the most richly carved with its pendants, one of which ends in the grinning face of a Green Man, and its famous Prentice Pillar, (110) stands as the background for the sacrifice of the Mass. The side aisles have lintelled tranverse vaults lit by six windows on each side, every one of which is surrounded by mouldings of luxuriant vegetation issuing out of the heads of Green Men. The Prentice Pillar is so called because of the legend, first recorded in the seventeenth century, associated with it. The master mason was told by his patron to build such a pillar but he felt he had to travel to Rome to learn how to construct it. While he was away it was built by his apprentice, who was told how to make it in a dream. His master, on returning, in a fit of jealous rage struck the apprentice dead with a blow of his mallet on the forehead.

A similar story is told of several churches and is of late currency but there are other links to stories of sacrifice, death and renewal. First, the Prentice Pillar is a representation of the sacred tree. On its capital is carved the story of the sacrifice of Isaac, a story that interpreted according to the levels of meaning mentioned earlier, signified the sacrifice of Christ for mankind, the sacrifice necessary in a life devoted to God, and the surrender of the soul to God. Round its base are eight dragons, their necks interlinked as out of their mouths issue the roots of the four swathes of vegetation that spiral round the pillar (111). They remind one both of the foliate beasts in Irish

110 *opposite. Roslin*. The Prentice Pillar *c*. 1450.

manuscripts that make interlace ornament in intricate patterns, and of the Norse legend, which would still have been alive and known in the Orkneys in the fifteenth century, of the world tree Yggdrasil whose roots are gnawed by the dragon of time. It was on this tree — as we saw earlier — that Odin sacrificed himself to gain wisdom. Here there are eight dragons, the number of renewal, that make the four spirals of vegetation — four being the number of wholeness: the Trinity and what it acts upon, the world — that in turn make the unity of the capital with its anagogic meaning in the story of Isaac of the union of the soul with God.

There is more. Next to that capital is a lintel of the south aisle carved with an inscription from the Book of Esdras which tells the story of the rebuilding of the Temple of Jerusalem by Zerubbabel in 515 BC — a story that must have had the deepest significance for the masons, going by the frequent references to the Temple in medieval accounts of the building of the cathedrals. The inscription comes from Zerubbabel's speech to King Darius for which he won the right to rebuild the temple. It translates: 'Woman is best but the truth will prevail beyond all.'[15]

Thus we find here the linking of strands from many sources of the theme of sacrifice and renewal. Central to all of them is, of course, the sacrifice of the Mass. It could look like a deliberate bringing together of Celtic, Scandinavian, Judaic and Christian variations on the same theme. Where does the Green Man fit into this and why does he recur so often? I have counted some ten Green Man heads including the pendant (112), just in the vicinity of the Prentice Pillar. Many of them have in their expressions something of the sinister grin on the face on the pendant. He reminds me of the Scottish tinker's story, that of the Green Man of Knowledge (pp.10–11) who, once met, sets you impossible tasks which you cannot accomplish without the help of his youngest daughter. The encounter with the Green Man of Know-

111 *Roslin*. The dragons round the base of the Prentice Pillar.

112 *Roslin*. The Green
Man on a pendant of the
retrochoir.

ledge can lead to a struggle to the death: the story is a parable of coming
face to face with deep creative powers within us. Through his daughter the
Green Man of Knowledge provides the means by which he may be overcome:
he wants to die but only at the hands of a worthy opponent just as the
energy within artistic inspiration cries out to be changed into a manifested
form if it is not to turn into a destructive force. It is interesting to apply
this thought to the legend of the Prentice Pillar. The master mason thought
he had to find that creative power by travel and study; his apprentice found
it at home by entering the Land of Enchantment in a dream and there he
learned to make the pillar. The thwarted desire of the mason caused him
to murder the apprentice and to destroy himself as an artist. If I am right
in thinking of the Green Man as the symbol to the masons of their inspiration
and creative power, then the Green Men of Roslin, taken in the context of
the themes of sacrifice and renewal, give us special savours, special warnings
of the dangers and triumphs within the desire to create.

Nowhere do the riddles of the Green Man appear more fully than in the
choirstalls of the Pyrenean cathedral of St-Bertrand de Comminges (116).
These are French Renaissance work by an international team of woodworkers
based on Toulouse, completed in 1535 and consecrated on Christmas Day

127

113 *St-Bertrand de Comminges*. St Michael conquers the devil who has a foliate head. Notice the Green Man on the Archangel's left knee.

114 *opposite. St-Bertrand de Comminges*. The Green Man as the foliate mask: two examples in contemplative *tête-à-tête* on armrests of the choirstalls, completed 1535.

by Bishop Jean de Mauléon. Although completely in the Renaissance style, the spirit of the symbolism of the choirstalls is thoroughly medieval, except for hints of the new magical philosophy of the Florentine Academy. There are more Green Men to the square foot of carving here than Clive Hicks or I have come across anywhere else.

To appreciate the impact of these choirstalls we must first say something of the cathedral in which they stand. The first sight of the chevet and tower of the cathedral placed on one of the foothills of the Pyrenees and with the steeply wooded sheer cliffs of mountains rising behind the cathedral is spectacular. The St Bertrand of its name was bishop here in the early twelfth century: he delivered the countryside from the depredations of a monstrous crocodile by touching its head with a walnut wand. Bertrand de Got, later Clement V, was also bishop here and one of the few good deeds of his life, blackened by his betrayal of the Templars and the flight of the Papacy to Avignon, was that he rebuilt the main body of the cathedral in the splendid open style of the *Gothique du Midi*, such was his veneration for his sainted namesake. At the same time or later, part of the Romanesque cloister was also rebuilt. Strange primitive Green Men are to be seen among the carvings here.

Life, you would think, was already as full as it could be with the glories of Nature and art as you mount towards the cathedral and enter by the side to see a mountainside of trees across the valley from the open arches of the cloister. The impact on entering the choir, however, to be dazzled by

116 St-Bertrand de Comminges. The cathedral lit at night.

115 opposite. St-Bertrand de Comminges. The Green Man and the Great Goddess: a winged woman, perhaps representing primal matter, gives birth to the head of a Green Man, on a misericord.

129

the rich, glistening golden browns of the choirstalls is to have wonder heaped on wonder — the work is of such beauty, feeling and craftsmanship.

The main themes of the choir seem to be these. The sides of the stalls facing the aisles are devoted to carvings and inlays of heroes such as the twelve worthies of antiquity. Everywhere in the fretted crestings and on the pilasters you will find Green Men in profile or as leaf masks or half figures rising out of vegetation as though here they symbolized the fruits of right action. The outside would therefore appear to signify the active life while the inner side of the choir, including the choirstalls with their carved backs, misericords, armrests, and raised ornamentation and figure carving, is devoted to the life of contemplation (114).

The panels above the upper stalls begin on the south side with a beautiful Annunciation. They continue with carvings of Old Testament prophets and representations of the virtues, saints and evangelists, the Tree of Jesse, other saints including St Bertrand, then the full sequence of the sibyls who foretold Christ and finally, facing the Virgin of the Annunciation, St Michael defeating Satan (113). The cosmic fall and victory over the rebel angels is answered across the choir by Gabriel appearing to Mary. When we look at the St Michael panel, we see not only that the Devil has a foliate head as though he were a Green Man but that St Michael's left knee — the one on which he advances towards the Devil — is made wholly of the head of a Green Man. The elemental powers that did not choose to follow Satan fight on the side of the good angels. That the foliate head appears both as good and evil is interesting in itself: that it is shown here in the context of primal creation and parallelled with the Incarnation demonstrates the continuity of two of the great themes with which the Green Man had been connected since the eleventh century.

Except for the Last Judgment, every other major context for the Green Man and nearly every associated image can also be found in the carvings at St-Bertrand de Comminges. The choirstalls could be looked upon as a deliberate act of recapitulation of the main images of Christian art over the preceding four centuries. Where the Green Man is concerned, he is here as an emblem of the function of the choir — which is the place of the utterance of praise. He is also to be found among numerous representations of the primal archetypal imagery associated with him — the snake or dragon, the sacred tree, the flower, the tree of Jesse, Adam and Eve standing on either side of *three* trees, and the Great Mother. He is also to be found as at Auxerre among the prophets and the sibyls who foretold Christ.

Here at St-Bertrand de Comminges is the only depiction I know of in which the Great Mother gives birth to the Green Man.[17] On a misericord in the centre of the south choirstalls is carved a naked woman: she is called a harpy in the guide books but she is a much greater creature than that. She has wings but no arms: leaves cover her shoulders where the arms would have protruded. Her feet are those of a frog. Her body is magnificently moulded and entirely female. As though she were a Delphic priestess contorting as the sacred bay leaves were burnt before her, her head rolls with the travail of birth. Between her thighs issues the smiling head of a Green Man (115).

If her wings signify air, her body earth, her batrachian feet water and her hair fire, then she can be seen as the fifth element, the primal matter from which ordered creation in the shape of the Green Man as Natural Law is born. She looks across at the other side to where Christ is tempted by the

117 opposite. St-Bertrand de Comminges. The Samian Sibyl holds a cradle as a prophecy of the Incarnation while a Green Man issues from the ground by her feet.

Devil offering to turn stones into bread. The Devil has the hideous face of the conventional medieval Devil but in place of his genitalia a man's face, scowling, is carved, signifying the level of fallen humanity that thinks entirely from its loins. It is an emblem of what the meaning of the choirstalls as a whole is intended to raise us above — to a level of thought and contemplation in which we are capable of receiving the wisdom of eternal ideas and images. It is in this mood that the spirit of the Renaissance and of the Florentine philosophers reigns so fully in the carvings and the space between them. It is also to be seen in the carving of the heads of most of the figures in the panels: there is an extraordinary emphasis given to the foreheads of these figures, whether they are of saints, of angels as with St Michael, or of prophets and prophetesses as with the sibyls. This emphasis on intellectual power and wisdom is also to be seen in the foreheads of the Green Men.

The Great Mother giving birth to the Green Man also looks across at the sibyls, among whom we find the Samian sibyl holding a cradle (117), thus prefiguring and prophesying the Incarnation. At her feet, growing out of the ground, rises the head of a Green Man smiling as a young tree emerges from the crown of his skull.

These are the great themes with many resemblances to earlier contexts in which the Green Man is shown. There are many other examples of him here in which the narrative is less easy to elucidate. Thus, what are we to make of the sequence of misericords that begins with a bare skull beneath the scene of the Annunciation, that follows in order with the head of a cherub with foliage issuing from his mouth, the head of a warrior, a Green Man, a woman with floating hair, another Green Man, the Great Goddess giving birth to the Green Man, with on the other side of her two monsters with the heads of Green Men? The sequence continues round the choir with scenes that evoke struggle, fulfilment, delight, further effort, and consummation in a garden where a couple, both naked, are seated. The woman hands the man a bough of the Tree of Life (illustration p. 164). It is as though the Green Man is included here in a journey, not through time to the Last Judgment but on a quest of interior transformations and trials to a recovery of the lost Paradise. We find that we have been led to happiness through the garden of the soul.

The garden, as a symbol of paradise, as a recreation of the groves of Academe where the Platonic philosophers once wandered, and as a place of refreshment and solace, was one of the great gifts of the Renaissance to civilization. Its symbolism had an appeal that was to cut across the religious divisions that had already broken out at the time that these choirstalls were being carved. Just as Neo-Platonic philosophy provided the stabilizing and unifying inspiration for Philip Sidney, Spenser and Shakespeare on one side of the religious divide and Titian, Michelangelo, Ronsard and du Bellay on the other, so the images and symbols that were nourished by that philosophy attained a universal circulation in art and architecture. With the cleverness and instinct for survival we have come to expect of him, the Green Man slipped out into the secular world among Renaissance ornamentation to discover new fields of enjoyment.

Chapter 7

Recurrences and Vanishings

On All Saints' Day 1517 Martin Luther nailed to the door of the castle church in Wittenberg the ninety-five theses that began the Reformation, thus splitting Western Christian society. Some years later Lucas Cranach the Elder painted a portrait of Luther as part of an altarpiece in Wittenberg (118). Cranach shows Luther standing in a stone pulpit; on the face of the pulpit is carved a foliate sea monster that combines the characteristics of a wild boar and a Leviathan. The tail of the monster is made of fronds terminating in the head of a Green Man.[1] It is no isolated connexion of the Green Man with Luther: many of his works printed at Wittenberg bear the Green Man on their title pages (119). There are few more striking instances than these to show how the Green Man slips across from one age of history to another.

In the Dark Ages we saw the Christian missionaries leading the attack on tree worship and thereby bringing about the psychic revolution in the attitudes to Nature from which Western science and technology sprang. In the Romanesque and Gothic periods the Church, having conquered the pagan past and encouraged the development of thought, particularly through scholastic theology, allowed and blessed the continuance of many formerly pagan practices in country and town life. The Green Man became an instrument of harmony between the pagan past and the Christian present, between the old myth-based participatory cultures and the new discovery by Western man of the powers of his own intellect, and between the laws of Nature and the laws of humanity. The stern leaders of the Reformation disturbed that balance by attempting to crush the popular ceremonies such as those of May Day in which much of the old vegetation rituals survived. Much of what we know about the folk rituals and dramas of the sixteenth and seventeenth centuries comes in fact from the denunciations of Protestants such as Bishop Latimer describing how no one would come to hear him preach a service because the Robin Hood plays were being performed.[2] Similarly Philip Stubbes, the Puritan chronicler, wrote thus of country ceremonies:

> Against May, Whitsunday, or other time, all the young men and maids, old men and wives, gadding over night to the woods, groves, hills and mountains, where they spend all night in pleasant pastimes; and in the morning they return, bringing with them birch and branches of trees to deck their assemblies withal. And we marvel, for there is a great Lord present amongst them, as superintendent and Lord over their pastimes and sport, namely Satan, prince of Hell. But the chiefest jewel they bring from thence is their May-pole, which they bring home with great vene-

ration as thus. They have twenty or forty yoke of oxen, every ox having
a sweet nosegay of flowers placed on the tip of his horns; and these
oxen draw home this May-pole (this stinking Idol, rather) which is
covered all over with flowers and herbs, bound round about with strings
from the top to the bottom, and sometime painted with variable colours,
with two or three hundred men, women and children following it with
great devotion. And thus being reared up with handkerchiefs and flags
hovering on the top, they strew the ground round about, bind green
boughs about it, set up summer halls, bowers and arbours hard by it.
And then fall they to dance about it, like as the heathen people did
at the dedication of the Idols, whereof this is a perfect pattern, or rather
the thing itself. I have heard it credibly reported (and that *viva voce*)
by men of great gravity and reputation, that, of forty, three-score, or
a hundred maids going to the wood overnight, there have scarcely the
third part of them returned home again undefiled.[3]

The missionaries of the Dark Ages had replaced the tutelary deities of the
countryside with a host of saints who acquired many of the associations and
legendary associations of the gods they conquered. The Protestant reformers
were now displacing those saints because they saw them as an interposition
between man and the Godhead. Behind the success of Protestantism in the
North lay powerful economic forces which required an ever greater exploitation of natural resources: the extension of mining, the introduction of drain-
ing on a vast scale, the construction of canals, the rise of what was to become
the chemical industry — as well as the part played by Protestant Holland
and England in the exploitation arising from the newly discovered routes
to Africa and the Indies. All of these depended on a necessary divorce between
man and Nature in the course of which man became increasingly the manipu-
lator and violator of Nature. The object of all these endeavours was increased
productivity and fruitfulness which was to pay for the great houses of the
nobility — replacing the castles of the past — and the splendid town houses
of the merchant classes. As the Green Man moved into that secular world
he became a frequently used symbol of that fruitfulness: he is to be seen
in chimneypieces, panelling, furnishing, embroideries and bronzes. Not only
does he appear on armour, but he enters the age of gunpowder by forming
part of the decoration of cannon, fowling pieces and the stocks of pistols.
The success of Protestantism in other ways depended on the command
of the new learning by the reformers and on the new invention that spread
that learning, the printed book. The imaginative needs of the educated classes
of Europe were, as a result of the new learning, fed by the myths and legends
of Greece and Rome. The inner meaning of those myths was expounded
by the Renaissance Neo-Platonic philosophers whose works, as I said in the
last chapter, provided a common meeting ground for minds otherwise separated by the great religious divide. The Green Man became a symbol of the
fruits of learning on which all parties depended for their arguments — and
as an illustration of this point one only has to look through a series of printed
books of the sixteenth and the first half of the seventeenth centuries to be sure
of finding him on title pages (1 and 119) as with Luther's works, in the borders
of plates and as colophons to chapters.[4] He is to be seen in bibles, liturgical
works and tomes of theology. From the church as the Bible of the Poor which

119 The Green Man and the Reformation: the title page of Luther's appeal to a General Council, Wittenberg 1520.

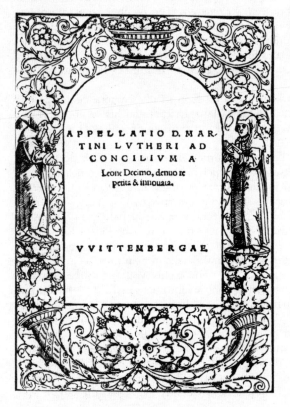

APPELLATIO D. MARTINI LVTHERI AD CONCILIVM A

Leone Decimo, denuo repetita & innouata.

VVITTEMBERGAE

118 *Wittenburg*. Luther preaching by Cranach the Elder: from the predella of an altarpiece painted for the Town Church. Note the foliate boar on the pulpit with its tail ending in the head of a Green Man.

was the chief context of his manifestations in the Middle Ages, the Green Man now appears in the literature of Everyman his own Priest.

The Green Man appears in the sculpture, architecture, and printed books of North-West Europe because he was made part of the vocabulary of ornament established earlier by the artists and architects of the Renaissance in Italy, the seat of the new learning of which he was to become a symbol. It is interesting to note that there are no Green Men in Italian Gothic sculpture, that I know of, to compare with the notable examples in France, Germany, Spain, and the British Isles that I have described. He does not figure at all in the works of Giovanni Pisano. He enters strongly, however, into Renaissance art, partly perhaps because the artists found him in the Roman sculpture they studied so avidly , but also because of the return of a pattern we have noted already in the past: this pattern is the combination of a return to realism in the depiction of vegetation with a new presentation of the image of man. The combination is one we have seen in the reign of Augustus with the vegetation of the Ara Pacis and the realism of the Roman portrait bust — the period in which the foliate head was first carved — and, later, in the high Gothic period. Realism in the sculpture of vegetation — such as may be seen in the surrounds of Ghiberti's Baptistery doors at Florence — spread into the paintings drawing on the Tuscan and Umbrian landscapes. The themes of transformations drawn from Ovid's *Metamorphoses* took on a new immediacy with the realism of the leaves into which, for instance, the body of Daphne was changed, or the example given earlier (14) of the transformation of Chloris into Flora in Botticelli's *Primavera*. The theme of metamorphosis was also revived with the reintroduction of the inhabited scroll with its vegetation pouring out of the mouths of foliate heads and turning into the bodies of half figures, both male and female. These revivals of ornament combined with the new individualism of Renaissance portraiture could produce some remarkable images.

120 *Mantua*. Mantegna's self-portrait as a Green Man in the west wall of the Camera degli Sposi of the Ducal Palace, *c*. 1474.

One of the most remarkable is to be seen in the Camera degli Sposi in the Ducal Palace at Mantua, where Mantegna painted his self-portrait as a Green Man in one of the scrolls looking out at his glorification of the members of the Gonzaga family (120)[5].

Renaissance artists, while making important changes in their portrayal of the image, used him in the contexts which by this time had become traditional for him. He is to be seen in the context of praise in a frieze in the *cantoria* or singing gallery made for the Duomo in Florence by Donatello, who introduced a subtle variation by forming the faces out of palmettes. Donatello also set him in the context of the Passion as a row of foliate half-figures above his carving of the entombment on the pulpit in San Lorenzo (121). He also begins to appear in architectural details in paintings, as in Filippino Lippi's frescos in Santa Maria Novella and in his *Madonna with Four Saints* in the Uffizi. He is also to be seen in tomb sculpture, as in the design Filippino made for his father's tomb in Spoleto Cathedral. The greatest Florentine artist of all, Michelangelo, had a particular attachment to the foliate head and frequently drew and carved it or had it made according to his design. Thus we find the Green Man on the frame of the *Doni Madonna* (in the Uffizi), carved to Michelangelo's directions. He also had him carved for the tomb of Pope Julius II in Rome, and in his designs for the desks and lecterns of the Laurentian Library in Florence he frequently employed the Green Man

to express the fruits of learning that would be the rewards of those who studied in the library.

The most important appearance of the image in work from his own hand, apart from his drawings, is in the Medici Chapel. There he carved him on the front and back of the cuirass of Giuliano de' Medici, Duke of Nemours (122). That on the front of the cuirass in the traditional position of the heart is both winged and foliate, agonized and exalted at the same time in its expression. Beside the figure of Night lies a frightening mask with winged ears and bared front teeth. The baring of the teeth is multiplied many times in the frieze immediately behind in the row of foliate heads[6] that take on the character of tragic masks. These heads are repeated on the tomb of Lorenzo de' Medici opposite, and they form a grim chorus chanting strophe and antistrophe on the theme of mortality and the extinction of the renown of fame (123). Each head is separated by a dart, a motif taken up on the next level by the conventional egg-and-dart theme; but here the egg signifies rebirth, of which the assurance is confirmed by the gaze of both Giuliano and Lorenzo towards the Virgin and Child.

121 *Florence*. Foliate half-figures look down on the entombment of Christ: Donatello's last work, the pulpit in San Lorenzo, *c.* 1460 which was completed by Bertoldo.

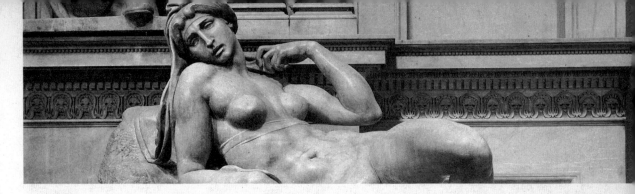

Knowledge of such masterpieces was spread by travelling artists and by books and engravings to other countries. Thus in his writings on architecture Sebastiano Serlio depicted the foliate head many times in engravings showing how to place and arrange decoration in buildings.[7] In the depictions of the Green Man from this period onward, because of the sources of the new art, he tended to swing naturally to his southern forebears, to Bacchus and his crew and to the armies of nymphs and satyrs now set free once more by artists and sculptors. Though, as we shall see, he continued to be carved and sculpted in tomb and church architecture, his secularization led to his demotion from the special place he had held in the estimation of Northern sculptors. He is only one among many images of fecundity and plenty that bring back the theme of the Golden Age. His depictions often take on the quality of a mask, so that he becomes a persona in the theatre of life rather than an intrinsic spirit. He loses some of the great significations of the beginnings of creation and the course and ending of time with which he had been associated in the Middle Ages. His special qualities are stolen for other images, such as the strange heads in which, instead of leaves issuing from the orifices of the head, cloths like shrouds hang out of the ears, eyes and mouths.[8] Or else he becomes a gigantic caricature, as with the heads that form the frames and doorways of the Palazzo Zuccari in Rome or the monsters in the Orsini garden at Bomarzo. On a smaller scale the extent to which the element of caricature debased his archetypal qualities may be seen in the extraordinary heads painted by Arcimboldo, frequently using the device of forming the features out of fruit and vegetables as in his two portraits of the alchemist Emperor Rudolph II, one as Vertumnus and the other as Autumn (124).

There are still fine examples of him to be seen from the early sixteenth century onwards. I have already described at length his multiple appearances in the new style at St-Bertrand de Comminges. At the very time that those choirstalls were being carved, other craftsmen were working on the screen of King's College Chapel in Cambridge, one of the earliest Renaissance works in England. There the Green Man is to be seen all along the front of the screen. In the same decade the finest of all the church roofs of Somerset was being erected at Shepton Mallet — again strongly influenced by the new style and again incorporating the Green Man several times in the carving of the panels. Even a Devon country church like High Bickington can provide thirty-seven examples of him in the new style.

If the Green Man loses much of the fineness of spirit and depth of symbolic meaning he expresses in so many of his Gothic depictions, we still have to account for his popularity and his ubiquity in the art and architecture of the sixteenth and seventeenth centuries. We know from Elizabethan

123 Florence. The frieze of foliate heads behind a detail of the statue of Dawn on the tomb of Lorenzo de' Medici in the Medici Chapel. *Mansell Collection.*

122 opposite. Florence. The tomb and statue of Giuliano de' Medici in the Medici Chapel on which Michelangelo worked 1520–4 and 1530–33. In addition to the foliate heads on Giuliano's cuirass and the frieze behind the statues of Night and Day there are others in the capitals above. *Alinari.*

139

124 Portrait of the
Emperor Rudolph II as
Autumn by Arcimboldo,
Museo Civico, Brescia.
Alinari.

accounts that he frequently appeared in masques and processions in the company of wild men and other grotesque figures. We have to presume largely from their later survival the practice of numerous seasonal rituals in which the May King, the Feuillu, the Pfingstl and the Green Man participated.

For what the Green Man meant in this period and why he was so popular as an image of fecundity, we can turn to literature. Though there is no description of the Green Man in Rabelais, it is in the generous, ebullient *gauloiserie* of *Gargantua et Pantagruel*, the feeling of the earth and the enjoyment of her produce, the exultant acknowledgement of the needs, functions and senses of the body, the abundance of words and the celebration of enjoyment, that we find a similar spirit to that of the muscular caryatids, the full-breasted nymphs and the foliate heads among the swags of fruit and flowers in the decoration of the palaces and chateaux of the time of Francis I and Henry II of France. The origin of Rabelais' work is the Celtic legend of the outrageously randy giant Grangousier and it is significant to see that a similar revival of Celtic themes took place in Tudor England at the same time, encouraged, of course, by the fact that the new dynasty of the Tudors was Welsh in origin. The most notable return of Cernunnos as the demon of Windsor Great Park, Herne the Hunter, is to be found in Shakespeare's *Merry Wives of Windsor*. There Mistress Page tells her fellow conspirators as they plot to punish Falstaff

There is an old tale goes that Herne the Hunter,
Sometime a keeper here in Windsor forest,
Doth all the winter-time, at still midnight,
Walk round about an oak, with great ragg'd horns;
And there he blasts the tree, and takes the cattle
And makes milch-kine yield blood, and shakes a chain
In a most hideous and dreadful manner.[9]

Related themes appear in the works of other dramatists. Thus we find George Peele making use of the Celtic cult of the head and its association with wells in *The Old Wives' Tale*. Celanta dips her pitcher into a well and a voice speaks:

> Gently dip but not too deep
> For fear you make the golden beard to weep.

A head comes up with ears of corn which she combs into her lap.

> Fair maiden, white and red
> Comb me smooth and stroke my head;
> And thou shalt have some cockell bread.
>   Gently dip but not too deep,
>   For fear thou make the golden beard to weep.

Then a head full of gold arises and this too she combs into her lap.

> Fair maiden, white and red,
> Comb me smooth and stroke my head;
> And every hair a sheave shall be
> And every sheave a golden tree.[10]

Peele took this incident from the old story of *The Princess of Colchester*. Peele was particularly sensitive to the resonances of ancient traditions, which is evidenced by his knowledge of the part played by sacred trees as when in *David and Bethsabe* Absalom utters the glorious lines

> God in the whizzing of a pleasant wind
> Shall march upon the tops of mulberry trees.[11]

Peele also in his *Edward I* (1593) introduced a Robin Hood play, performed by Lluellen, the last Prince of Wales, with his companions while hiding in the mountains.

The Robin Hood play is referred to or incorporated in several other Elizabethan plays. It would seem to have been a performance of great popularity from Scotland to Cornwall, and Robin Hood became associated with the annual choosing of the Summer Lord and the May Queen.[12]

It was part of a world that the young John Milton was to immortalize in his *L'Allegro* and which in England was to receive a shock from the coming Civil War, from which it never truly recovered. When in his ode *On the Morning of Christ's Nativity*, written when he was only twenty-one, Milton described the effect of the Incarnation upon the gods of the Mediterranean world, he was also uttering a prophecy of the extinction of the old participatory country culture and belief structure of England.

The lonely mountain o'er,
And the resounding shore,
  A sound of weeping heard and loud lament;
From haunted spring and dale,
Edged with poplar pale,
  The parting Genius is with sighing sent.[13]

It is remarkable that Milton and his friend and colleague Andrew Marvell, both of them champions of the Commonwealth and the new regime, should have articulated so clearly the attractions of the old order — more clearly in many ways than poets on the other side of the quarrel such as Robert Herrick. Both men were exceptionally responsive to sensual impressions and could charge their language with that responsiveness, while at the same time their thought processes were developed to the highest degree in the following out of a line of logical thought and in the compression of thought and experience into compact verse. The word 'green' was to Marvell a poem in itself: his works resonate with its repetitions. He entered into it as into the union of a mystical illumination — as when he wrote of 'The Garden':

Annihilating all that's made
To a green Thought in a green Shade.[14]

It was probably from the same experience that gave him those lines that in another poem he described himself turning into a Green Man. The poem 'Upon Appleton House, to my Lord Fairfax' was written in the period when Marvell was tutor to Mary Fairfax, daughter of the renowned Parliamentary commander in the Civil War. The poem is at once a tribute to his patron and a celebration of the works of man and of Nature as seen in Fairfax's estate, which stands as a microcosm of the universe and of mind. It is also a love poem. The climax of the work is a paean of praise to his pupil Mary, who is the goddess that gives the gardens their beauty, the woods their 'straightness', the meadows their sweetness, and the river its purity:

She yet more Pure, Sweet, Straight, and Fair
Then Gardens, Woods, Meads, Rivers are.[15]

To achieve this revelation of Mary as the guiding genius of the place, Marvell himself has gone on a gently disguised allegorical journey in the course of the poem. The meadows are flooded, so he goes into the wood:

But I, retiring from the Flood
Take Sanctuary in the Wood;
And, while it lasts, myself imbark
In this yet green, yet growing Ark . . . [16]

Using the ancient symbolism of the wood as the human mind, he describes the trees and birds he sees there and enters a state where he understands the language of Nature:

Out of these scatter'd Sibyl's Leaves
Strange *Prophecies* my Phancy weaves:
And in one History consumes,
Like *Mexique Paintings*, all the *Plumes*.
What *Rome, Greece, Palestine*, ere said
I in this light *Mosaick* read.

Thrice happy he who, not mistook,
Hath read in *Natures mystick Book*.[17]

Then the poet turns into the Green Man:

And see how Chance's better Wit
Could with a Mask my studies hit!
The Oak-Leaves me embroyder all,
Between them Caterpillars crawl
And Ivy, with familiar trails,
Me licks, and clasps, and curles, and hales.
Under this antick Cope I move
Like some great *Prelate of the Grove*.[18]

The wind purifies his thoughts, winnowing 'from the Chaff my Head'.
He feels utterly safe behind the trees where his mind is now encamped.
The world is powerless to touch him while he himself can play on it. Neverthe-
less he makes this plea:

Bind me ye Woodbines in your 'twines,
Curle me about ye gadding *Vines*,
And Oh so close your Circles lace
That I may never leave this Place
But, lest your Fetters prove too weak,
Ere I your Silken Bondage break,
Do you, *O Brambles*, chain me too,
And Courteous *Briars* nail me through.[19]

Whether he knew of the image from carvings in churches, such as those
at Beverley Minster near where he grew up at Hull, or from folk customs
and plays or from masques, or whether the archetypal associations rose up
in him while he contemplated the image, cannot be told. The fact is that
Marvell recreates here through his own experience many of the themes that
we have seen are common to the image of the Green Man, direct knowledge
of the wisdom of Nature, inspiration, prophecy, priesthood and, most
especially, love of the Goddess. Here the image of the Green Man contributes
to, and is interpreted in the light of, Neo-Platonic philosophy as an image
of the state in which the poet becomes open to all knowledge of man and
of Nature through what he describes elsewhere as

The Mind, that Ocean where each kind
Does streight its own resemblance find.[20]

Marvell draws out from the image the immensity of meanings which the
Gothic sculptors had found in it and which had narrowed with the secularization of the image in more recent years. A story from Wales told by a poet
who fought on the Royalist side, Henry Vaughan, also expresses the theme
of inspiration.

I was told by a very sober and knowing person (now dead) that in his
time there was a young lad fatherless and motherless, and so very poor
that he was forced to beg; but at last was taken up by a rich man that
kept a great stock of sheep upon the mountains not far from the place
where I now dwell, who clothed him and sent him into the mountains

to keep his sheep. There in summertime, following the sheep and looking to their lambs, he fell into a deep sleep, in which he dreamed that he saw a beautiful young man with a garland of green leaves upon his head and a hawk upon his fist, with a quiver full of arrows at his back, coming towards him (whistling several measures or tunes all the way) and at last let the hawk fly at him which he dreamed got into his mouth and inward parts, and suddenly awaked in a great fear and consternation, but possessed with such a vein, or gift of poetry, that he left the sheep and went about the Country, making songs on all occasions, and came to be the most famous Bard in all the Country in his time.[21]

Marvell's poems created no great stir when they were published after his death in 1681, and Vaughan's story was in a private letter not printed till many years later. There was, however, a story with the widest circulation that may well have contributed to the continuing popularity of the Green Man image, and that is the story of Charles II and Boscobel Oak.

After the battle of Worcester in 1653 when Cromwell had routed the Royalist forces and the young Charles II, claimant to the throne, was forced to flee, at one point in his adventures he had to hide in the branches of a tree called Boscobel Oak while the Parliamentary soldiers searched for him underneath. Charles was known at the time by the sobriquet of the Black Boy, and the associations with the decapitation of his father like one of the sacrificed kings of old, the holy and protective nature of the oak, and the ability of the young prince to change his shape like one of the ancient heroes added to the thrill of the story. At the Restoration Charles II returned like the Summer Lord, in May, to be greeted with processions and crowds waving oak branches. The old games and rituals were revived as an expression of loyalty. At Nottingham a special version of the Robin Hood play was performed in which at the end Robin Hood and his men made submission to royal authority.[22] After the Restoration the oak leaf continued to be a symbol of the Royalist party and many inns were given the name 'The Royal Oak.' A popular form for the inn sign would be an oak with its foliage filled with the crowned head of Charles II, and this form may have owed much to the traditional representations in churches of the Green Man.

That story may account for the renewed popularity of the image in later seventeenth-century England. It cannot explain why throughout Europe architects and sculptors of the Baroque style continued to use the image. The obvious explanation is that the vitality of the foliate head accorded well with the exuberance of the Baroque style: what finer climax could be found for rusticated bark-like blocks of stone cut round arches than the Green Man in the keystones, and what more suitable visage than his could bloom in the bold sinuosities of the balustrades mounting a staircase? With the development of garden architecture and sculpture he was found new and suitable uses. In church architecture and furnishings of the seventeenth century he kept many of his old associations. To take examples noted on our more recent travels, he appears as an emblem of praise in the choirstalls of Moissac, of Toulouse Cathedral, and of St-Sernin at Toulouse: in Denmark we found him in the balustrade of the pulpit in Nyborg church as an emblem of eloquence and on the metal casings of the royal tombs in Roskilde Cathedral as an emblem of resurrection. In Scotland he became a popular device for

125 *opposite. London.* One of the Green Men in the choir screens of St Paul's cast by Jean Tijou for Sir Christopher Wren, 1695–7.

carving on tombstones because he seemed to bear none of the associations of popery conveyed by conventional Christian imagery.

Sir Christopher Wren would appear to have loved the Green Man. He was carved in many places in St Paul's, and Tijou cast his face for the choir screens of the Cathedral (125). (When the rood screen and organ were removed from the front of the choir in the 1890s to open up the vista to the high altar, the design of the low metalwork screen that took their place was also centered on the Green Man.) A year ago I was invited to lecture at Croydon: the Green Man was a linking theme in the lectures. To collect my thoughts before speaking I had gone for a short walk and found myself opposite a fine late seventeenth-century mansion, suitably called Wrencote House. Looking up at the eaves I saw some five particularly expressive Green Men gazing back as though to give me encouragement. Shortly afterwards, I passed through Queen Anne's Gate, a journey I have made hundreds of times, and I realized that the sculptures on the keystones were nearly all of Green Men, Green Men scowling, grinning, melancholic, minatory and indifferent. The houses to which they give such varied life were built around 1704 (126 and 127). When additions were made to Queen Anne's Gate earlier this century in an attempt to follow the style of the older houses the new keystones were carved with heads — but not with Green Men: they are gloomy pseudo-classical faces with none of the vitality of their older fellows, as though the significance of the image had entirely escaped architect, patron and sculptor.

The Green Man continued to be popular in the first part of the eighteenth century. One of the finest representations of the period is at Tewkesbury in the Gage Gates to the Abbey. Tewkesbury Abbey possesses one of the best sequences of medieval Green Men bosses in England. When Lord Gage, formerly MP for the town, presented these wrought-iron gates in 1734, the smith, challenged by the older images, outdid himself to produce a Green Man for the top of the arch to welcome worshippers to the Abbey.[23]

With changes in style and understanding in the later eighteenth century the Green Man went to sleep again in art and architecture. The one place where he survived was the garden. It might be thought that after so many centuries of prodigal expenditure of energy he had retired to contemplate calm lakes from garden urns or to refresh his powers by gazing down avenues of trees from quiet temples. But if he seemed to be resting, it was a delusion. He was there in the gardens not merely to give them an antique charm but because of what was happening in his particular kingdom of the plants. In a way and on a scale never known before, the plants of the world were being analysed and classified by Linnaeus and his followers: ardent explorers hunted exotic plants, and artists travelled thousands of miles to record new discoveries. The Royal Gardens at Kew were to become one of the great centres of research into his world, and in the next century the Green Man was to be set in the main gates of the gardens (128) occupying a place of honour as formerly he had been placed at the entrances to cathedrals.

Where art and architecture are concerned it may be that he disappeared not just because as an image he was unsuited to the decoration of neo-classical buildings but because of the effect of the combination of the rational-scientific attitude with the exploitative technology of the Industrial Revolution. An image of balance between man and Nature such as the Green Man was as unsuitable to a scientist such as the Reverend Robert Hales at Teddington,

126 *London*. Queen Anne's Gate *c*. 1704 with its keystones of Green Man heads.

127 *London*. One of the Green Man heads in Queen Anne's gate.

conducting his experiments into plant physiology, as it would have been to the mine and mill owners of the industrial North. They were exploiting energy from coal, a source known for centuries but never before used on such a scale, for their pumping houses and machinery. They and the chemical manufacturers were beginning the process of pollution which we till recent years have come to accept as a natural and unavoidable consequence of industrial development. The coal mines also supplied the fuel for heating and cook-

147

ing which enabled the rapid expansion of the big cities and industrial towns of late eighteenth- and nineteenth-century England.

And here we meet a puzzle. From the 1780s onwards on May Day the chimney sweeps would dress up and dance in the street around a figure entirely encased in leaves known as the Jack in the Green or Jack of the Green, who bobbed and nodded with the dance. Some of the earlier writers on the Green Man identified the Green Man in churches with the Jack in the Green and presumed that the Jack went back in time to the pre-industrial era. Roy Judge, however, in his study of the Jack in the Green, has found no definite illustration of him before 1795, though there are possible references to him *c*.1775-85.[24] From the early nineteenth century onwards there is a host of illustrations, references in literature and reminiscences to show that it was a custom based on London spreading out through Southern and Midland England. Emigrants were to take the custom far afield so that it is recorded as being performed in Tasmania, for example. At a later stage the Jack in the Green was incorporated into May Day celebrations independently of the sweeps' parades in the possibly mistaken belief, fired by antiquarian zeal, that it had a rightful place in the ceremonies. The dance of the sweeps was performed in many places well into this century.

If it was — as seems certain from the evidence — a custom that rose up only during the period of the Industrial Revolution, it arouses many questions. The custom of dressing a man in a wicker framework covered with leaves is one with many parallels from accounts of older rituals, but why did the sweeps do it and why was it so particularly a custom practised in towns? The custom appears at a period when the Green Man as an image in art and architecture went into abeyance, and yet it is connected in the deepest levels with the forest world of the Green Man. The sweeps were from the lowest strata of society and it was their job to clean up the mess made by the coal that derived from the great forests of the Carboniferous Era of geological time. They could, of course, have known nothing of the origins of coal, but nevertheless they and the unfortunate children whom they drove up the chimneys depended for their livelihood on the energy of ancient sunlight preserved in dead and petrified vegetation; and once a year they danced around a figure encased in living vegetation as a symbol of life and renewal. Is this an example of an archetypal force arising in the popular consciousness as a counterbalance to the misery and grime of life in industrialized society? And, if so, is it the same archetypal force that has at so many times in history given rise to its artistic and dramatic expression as the lover of the Goddess, the Green Man, and the variations of the foliate head? The Jack in the Green is contemporary with the eruption of a much greater archetypal power: the sacred tree reborn as the Tree of Liberty of the French Revolutionaries. The significance of this, together with the relationship of Romanticism and the rise of science to the Green Man, is dealt with in the next chapter.

As surprising as the appearance of the Jack in the Green in this period is the comparative absence of the Green Man from the sculpture of Gothic Revival churches in England in the Victorian period. There may be many reasons for this: one that, being ardent readers of medieval writers on the symbolism of church architecture such as Durandus, the ecclesiologists and architects could find no reference to him that would sanction his revival; another that they regarded him as a pagan figure and therefore to be excluded

128 *opposite. London*. The Green Man with the expression of a whiskered Victorian scientist: from the main gates of Kew Gardens designed by Decimus Burton, 1843.

149

129 *London*. Looking down on Richard the Lion-Heart from high up on the Palace of Westminster are Green Men. It is typical of the image that it should manifest in buildings that sum up the concentrated energies of an age. Thus it appears in the Houses of Parliament, the most notable architectural expression of constitutional government, by Sir Charles Barry and A. W. N. Pugin.

like all the unsavoury carvings they must have often seen in their explorations of old churches. The masons of Chartres had transformed the image of the Green Man by synthesizing their knowledge of how to portray the human head with their skill in carving vegetation. The Victorian sculptors had little urge to bring these elements together. Too much of the ecclesiastical figure sculpture of the period is characterized by a tame nobility that leaches the dramas of the soul inherent in the stories of the saints and apostles that are portrayed. They have the mouths of children who are good because they have no energy to be bad. Victorian Gothic leaf carving, though it may impress by its detail and observation, has the flavour of the botanical plate: it lacks symbolic depth. There are, however, exceptions: in St Stephen's, Rochester Row, in Westminster, not only are the leaf capitals of superb quality but in the south aisle there is a fine corbel of a Green Man.

When restoring medieval churches and buildings, the architects were often scrupulous in replacing worn or battered Green Man heads — probably more so in France than in England or Germany. Thus the towers of Angers Cathedral are surrounded high up by the heads of Green Men, quite clearly nineteenth-century in execution but presumably replacing earlier examples. Viollet-le-Duc also knew and loved the image and would have it carved to his direction. I could not see any trace of the Green Man on the west front of Cologne Cathedral, entirely constructed in the last century. On the other hand, Sir Gilbert Scott in rebuilding the west front of St David's Cathedral had a Green Man carved over the door, copied from the worn twelfth-century example over the north door of the nave. If the image was not in general thought proper for churches, it was often allowed for secular buildings. Thus Pugin permitted it to be carved along the upper string courses of the Palace of Westminster above the statue of Richard the Lionheart (129) and round the base of the Victoria Tower. You will also find Green Men in the nineteenth-century rebuilding or recarving of Oxford colleges.

By denying themselves the archetypal power of the Green Man, the architects of the Gothic Revival cut themselves off from a great potential source of inspiration for their churches. Though they frequently achieved new and beautiful orderings of space in their development of the Gothic style as well as in their use of polychrome work to enliven their surfaces, they never saw that there was an essential link between man and Nature to be explored in the image.

But why did the Green Man return with the revival of Renaissance and Palladian styles of architecture from the 1870s onwards when he had been ignored in the Gothic Revival? It is easy to see where the architects and craftsmen found him: in works like Owen Jones's *Grammar of Ornament*. It is not so easy to say why he became so popular again. The Wren style was

130 *London*. The Green Man in ceramic work on 28 South Audley Street.

revived in a fashionable movement, partly aroused by Thackeray's *Henry Esmond*. Revivals of Elizabethan and Jacobean models for country and town houses had been popular since Salvin, and a growing admiration for the Quattrocento had led to the construction of numerous *palazzi* for clubs and public buildings. With the revival of these styles — to which one should add Dutch Renaissance — there came a fashion for the grotesqueries and fantastic designs that were common to their originals. They were developed farther through the popularity of ceramic architecture: the great red panels of moulded clay that lent themselves so well to foliage and faces. Triumphing among all these styles you will find the Green Man.

If you wander round Mayfair looking for buildings of this period, you will discover the Green Man peeping out from walls, windows and door surrounds (130, 131 and 132). There is a permanent riot of ceramic Green Men on the houses close to the University Women's Club. Bond Street and its side streets offer examples as rich in variety as the contents of the shops. And furthermore he now appears in greater numbers in secular buildings of the Gothic revival, such as the extraordinary Perpendicular-style bank that crouches in the shadow of the Dorchester Hotel. Lined along the string courses are Green Men looking out at Hyde Park.

Cernunnos, it must be remembered, was the god of wealth as well as of the underworld and it was perhaps in this guise, quite unknown to those who carved or moulded the Green Man, that he became a symbol of the late Victorian commercial spirit. He also appears among the fantastic decorations of public houses built in the Flemish Renaissance style such as The World's End in Chelsea, as well as in Wren revival buildings such as Chelsea Town Hall. It is, in its way, as striking an example of the archetypal force of the image returning as the Jack in the Green of the sweeps — all the more so because it also arises in an urban and industrialized setting.

I take these examples from parts of London where I habitually pass. Any of my readers who live close to later nineteenth-century buildings of these syncretic styles, whether in Western Europe or in North America, can probably match the examples I have given. New York possesses numerous instances of the image, for example the carvings by Thomas Graham at 24 East 95th Street (*c*.1899) and by Oswald Wirz on 56-8 Pine Street (1893).[25] Then from the 1920s there follows extinction — extinction not only for the Green Man but for all decorative and figure sculpture on buildings. The thought that a building ought to have its meaning and spirit expressed in ornamentation that was integral to its design was no longer to be entertained. Men were machines and therefore buildings should be considered as machines for housing machines. Decoration was expensive and, on the grounds of a new intellectual aestheticism that disliked decoration, it could be dispensed with. So architects, in alliance with Mammon, committed mass aesthetic suicide. The economic forces that, unwittingly, the Protestant reformers had released with their attacks on the restraints on usury and the old participatory culture of the past had triumphed, leading to a blind materialism and unthinking uglification.

The Green Man went to sleep again.

132 *London*. Another foliate face from 23 Albemarle Street.

131 *opposite*. *London*. An art-nouveau Green Man in ceramic work on 23 Albemarle Street.

153

Chapter 8

The Green Man returns

In one of the most delightful and enduring works inspired by the Celtic Revival, *The Crock of Gold*, James Stephens tells how the Philosopher, after spending the night in the cave of the God Aengus Óg, comes across a boy. He asks the boy his name and is told it is MacCushin. He says that Aengus Óg had told him that if he met a boy called MacCushin he should tell him, 'The Sleepers of Erin have awoken.' He goes on to say that, though he is old, MacCushin is young and the boy's mission will be to greet the Sleepers and to tell them their names and lineage because they have forgotten them. It is essential that they should be reminded who they are and be greeted as friends. The boy understands immediately. 'I shall make a poem some day,' he says, 'and every man will shout when he hears it!'[1]

The Green Man is one of those Sleepers. But while he slept, he also dreamed in preparation for his return and his dreams filtered into the dreams of musicians and composers.

Wagner rediscovered the voice of myth in music. In doing so he revealed new resources of sound through which the emotions of Nature and the intertwining of man's fate could be expressed. He gave his successors all over Europe and North America a fresh orchestral palette with which they could paint the spirit of country and landscape in sound. This coincided with the revival of interest in folk song, music, dance and lore in the exploration of which many composers such as Bartok and Vaughan Williams were to take part. Greenmans, the country world of our image, was recorded and set down at the very time when for the most part its culture was to be destroyed by urbanization, war and the mechanization of farming. Music that was inspired by particular landscapes and folk songs and rhythms, music that re-established the identity of suppressed nationalities as in the case of Smetana and Dvorak for what was to become Czechoslovakia, and as in the case of Sibelius for Finland, or music that expressed the most ancient, nostalgic and poignant associations of man and landscape as in the works of Mahler, Vaughan Williams and Benjamin Britten, all this music arose from a sense of the basic emotional unity between man and the moods and forms of Nature — an idea so foreign to the dominant scientific and cultural philosophies of the period that it could only be expressed and find a wide audience through the language of music.

It is in a work by Vaughan Williams that we hear the voice of another Sleeper who wakes up: in his *Pastoral Symphony* composed during and after his experiences in the First World War he painted in sound the lost world of the Great Goddess, first in resounding and repeated phrases that make her ancient hills rise in the hearer's mind, then as her landscapes in spring

154

and summer, and finally simply as a woman's voice that goes on singing after the orchestra is silent.

The Great Goddess has returned, during the course of this century in many ways, often seemingly quite unconnected, through the recovery of myth and through the gradual realization of the matriarchal nature of the first farming communities, through the reassertion of the rights of women in politics, work and social life, through popular religion such as the promulgation of the Doctrine of the Assumption and the many recorded appearances of the Virgin, through the current debates on the role of women in the Church, in art (to which I will return later) and, most interestingly for our present purposes, in science.

The word matter — which is the subject of the investigations of science — comes from the same root as mother. For many centuries matter and its organized living forms in Nature have been treated by the largely male profession of scientists as their playthings, as the unconscious recipients of their violations and intrusions. Was it chance though that brought about the rise of a new branch of science that introduced the imagery of the feminine and of the generative bond of the sexes into the consideration of the workings of Nature? Was it chance also that caused this branch of science to arise at the same time that so many composers were expressing a new feeling for Nature in their works? This branch of science is ecology — etymologically the study of the housecraft of Nature, and by definition, the science of the interdependence of living things and their interreactions with their environments. It arose from the study, not only of plants and animals in relation to their geological and climatic environments, but also from the study of succession — the natural cycles by which, for example, grassland gives way to scrub and scrub to woodland and forest, to be followed in turn with the natural decay of forests, by the return of the land to grass and the renewal of the cycle. Each stage in the cycle reaches a point of perfection known as climactic climax which is maintained by the dynamic equilibrium of all the plants, fungi, bacteria, parasites and animals contributing to the system. The rise of ecology brought about a major change in the thinking of many scientists: it turned them away from seeking truth through analysis, fragmentation, and the study of individual organisms isolated from their environments to looking for the whole systems within which an ecological balance is maintained. At first they studied parishes of plants and animals, and then regions. Then the Russian scientist Vladimir Vernadsky, drawing on the work of an earlier Austrian geologist, introduced in the 1920s the concept of the Biosphere to describe the film of living organisms that covers most of the surface of Earth, both land and ocean.[2] This concept has been reinforced recently by James Lovelock's Gaia hypothesis, according to which 'Earth's living matter, air, oceans, and land surface form a complex system which can be seen as a single organism and which has the capacity to keep our planet a fit place for life.'[3] With this hypothesis, influenced greatly by the study of Earth from outer space, the Great Goddess has returned bearing one of her ancient names, Gaia, the Greek for Mother Earth.

One of the consequences of the study of ecology has been an ever increasing sophistication in the awareness of the effect of humanity on the natural environment, more obviously through pollution studies but also in terms of the adaptations of Nature to the presence of humanity in more harmonious contexts. The pattern that I have so far suggested in this book is that there is a link between the Great Goddess and the Green Man and that, whenever she appears, he is likely to follow.

His return through scientific thought and imagery is, I think, still in its incipience but, before discussing that, I wish to consider a clearer emergence of the Great Mother-Green Man pattern, which is in certain developments in twentieth-century art.

Partly as a reaction against the masculine angularity of Cubism and partly inspired by the influence of Neolithic and other examples of prehistoric art, particularly of figures of the mother goddess, there appeared a new image in the work of many established and young artists in the later 1920s. This is the biomorphic form, a primordial rounded or curved shape, capable of being manipulated into a great variety of individual representations. It would seem to have arisen spontaneously among artists in Germany, France, Spain and England, in, for example, the work of Max Ernst, Jean Arp, Pablo Picasso, Yves Tanguy, Joan Miró and the young Henry Moore. It also appeared very early in the career of the twentieth-century artist whose works Clive Hicks and I have studied most deeply, Cecil Collins. From 1932 onwards he was painting a series of visionary works in which out of the maternal biomorphic form there emerge the shapes or heads of men. In *The Joy of the Worlds* (1937) a naked pilgrim with a staff is born in the midst of the white amniotic bubbles of a womb and the world all about is a radiant green (133).[5] In *The Voice* (1938) the biomorphic form breaks open as waves beat against it to reveal a great prophetic head.[6] It is significant that Collins was of Celtic Cornish background and that the Celtic veneration for the head as a prophetic instrument returned in his work. There is a quality in the essence of his heads which, I believe, comes closest in recent art to expressing the meaning of the Green Man image and to helping us to understand why he is coming back now. This quality is particularly to be seen in Collins's lithograph *Head* (1960),[7] in which many people have seen the image of the head as appearing through leaves, and in his later *Icon of Divine Light* painted for an altar front in Chichester Cathedral (1973).[8] The example of the theme in his work that we give here (134) is a drawing, *The Tree of Life* (1946), in which a stroke of lightning darts to earth creating a tree with a crown of five lobes — the number of Nature and man. Round the tree there forms the shape of a human head.

Other artists who have turned to the image include John Piper, both in his graphic work and in his stained glass made in collaboration with Patrick Reyntiens for the Wessex Hotel, Winchester. The extent to which the image has aroused the interest of contemporary artists was seen recently in the exhibitions organized by the environmental group Common Ground. Of all the modern portrayals of the Green Man I have seen none speaks so fully of a new meaning being released through his spirit as the great dish by the artist and potter Alan Caiger-Smith, (front cover and 136). The new meaning is to be read most clearly in the expression of the eyes. Art may help us to comprehend the power of the image on a new scale, a power that with the help of science we can see is immeasurably greater in potential even than the vision of its greatest representations in the Gothic period.

If we look at the elements of which the Green Man is the composite, the leaf and the human head from the viewpoint of the knowledge given us

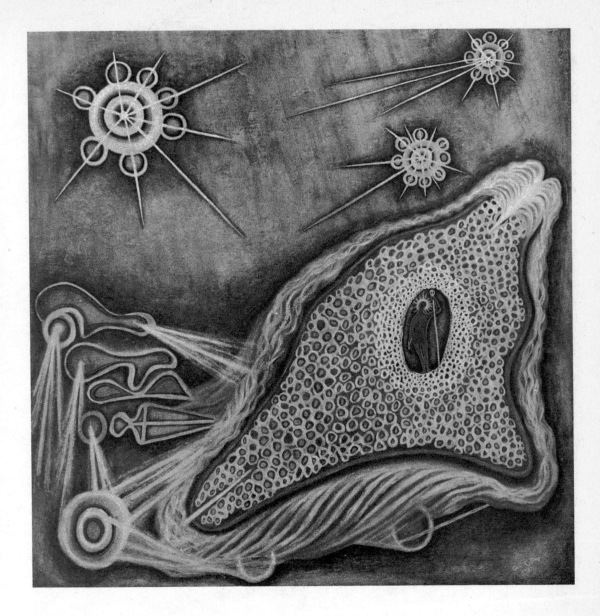

133 'The Joy of the Worlds' (1937) by Cecil Collins (1909–1989).

by science, we can try to grasp something of this scale. Through the discovery of photosynthesis we have learned more and more of the vital part played by the leaf in the creation and maintenance of the atmosphere in absorbing carbon dioxide and releasing oxygen. The leaf harvests the light of the sun to bring about the chemical reaction in its fluids that create the foods necessary for the continued growth of the plant of which it forms part. Through its veins circulate the juices drawn up from the rocks and the realms of the mole, the worm and the micro-organisms of the soil, to be touched in a series of instantaneous reactions by the light of the sun that at once convert carbon

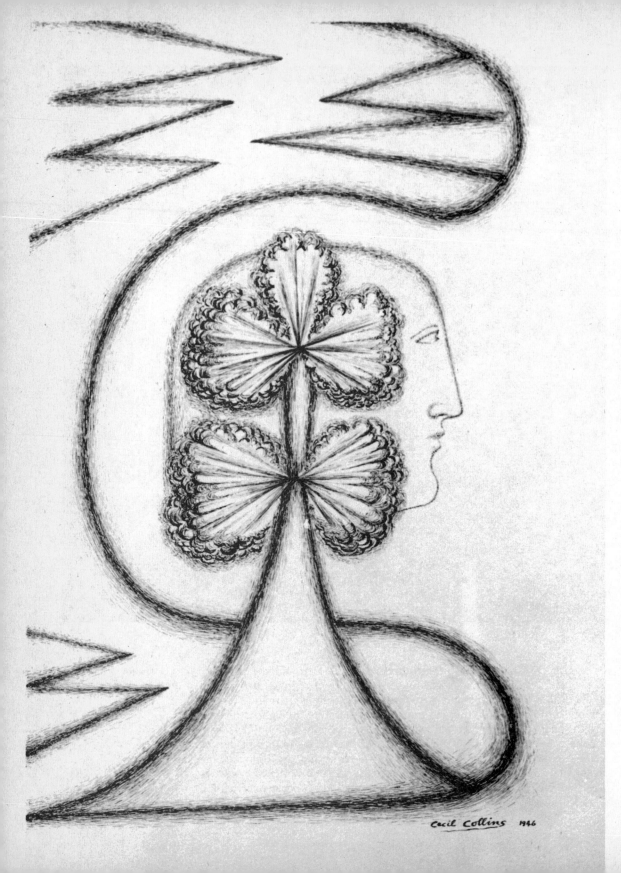

Cecil Collins 1946

dioxide and water into sugar for the growth of new cells and release both oxygen and water into the atmosphere, thus maintaining the balance which is part of the regulatory mechanisms of Gaia.

It was the German physician Jan Ingenhousz who in the late eighteenth century first saw the significance of the part played by the world of plants in maintaining the atmosphere. It was his contemporary, the founder of geology, James Hutton, who first compared the interconnexions between the crust, living organisms and atmosphere of the Earth to the circulation of the blood in the human body. It has taken a long time for their insights to grow and to be understood for their contributions to our knowledge of the workings of the biosphere and to the effect that man has had upon the global environment.

The reason why it has taken so long must be connected with the divisions that occurred between science, philosophy, art and religion with increasing sharpness from the later eighteenth century. It is as though the Green Man has had to undergo a period of retirement, similar to his seeming abeyance during the Dark Ages, because of the scale of the change in the attitude to Nature brought about from the period of the Industrial Revolution onwards. Though I have given many examples of how he survived during the nineteenth century, for the most part these look back to the past rather than create new contemporary meanings, and in Romantic art and literature we have to look for the currents that are contributory to his nature. Goethe and Coleridge are the most notable of the poets who could absorb the new science and contribute their own understanding to what it had to tell them, as Goethe did in his poems and writings on the metamorphosis of plants,[10] and as Coleridge bravely attempted in his philosophical writings.[11] Neither received much attention for his work, and a more general mood was expressed by Keats in his complaints about the dissection of the rainbow[12] and by Wordsworth, who looked on science as 'a succedaneum and a prop to our infirmity'.[13] It is in Wordsworth, though, that every now and then we get a direct statement that seems to come from the archetype of the Green Man, as with his 'One impulse from a vernal wood' and in the memories of the rocks, woods and streams that 'haunted him like a passion'.

134 *opposite.* 'The Tree of Life' (1946) by Cecil Collins.

The division between science and art reflects the increasing separation of people from their roots in the country through large-scale migration to industrial cities. The dark side of the Green Man, represented by the unbridled Dionysos and the vengeful Wotan, was unleashed as atavistic forces in the wars of this century. Though Friedrich Nietzsche gave brilliant expression to the Dionysos force and Wagner attempted a redemptive reinterpretation of Wotan, the powers of the neglected archetype were too great to be controlled. The green of life was not enriched with the gold of civilization. The fault lay not in the archetype but in humanity — because the archetype in its highest form expresses unity.

That unity may now be expressing itself in a new form. If the Great Goddess has appeared in science as the concept of Gaia then, going back to the founding myth, we must ask who the Green Man is in his new incarnation. He can be seen as the child of Gaia by the sun: he is the living face of the earth; and he has to utter. One of the proudest claims of science is that of successful prediction, based on reason, observation and the knowledge of causes. As our forefathers believed their prophets, priests, shamans and druids, so we believe the predictions of scientists — they are our prophets and when they predict the dangers threatening the world of the Green Man through the destruction of the rainforests, through environmental pollution and through the greenhouse effect, we pay attention and we tremble. Their predictions and our awareness of the threats have arisen because of the new nature and scale of the communication of information about the condition of the earth as a whole. Seen only in recent years for the first time from outside herself, earth has revealed many secrets about the interrelationships of her crust, her garment of living organisms, her atmosphere, and her magnetic field.

What new images, what new secrets has science uncovered in the human head, the other part of the Green Man's composite image? Science and its related technologies have taught us to think of it in terms of radio, of computers, of networks of nerve communications, of the transduction of electrical energy into chemical energy, of circuits, of brain waves and rhythms and of memory itself as a field phenomenon. We receive and we transmit through our heads. We seem to be genetically endowed with the ability to master the complex grammatical forms of language from our earliest days. We are born with two hemispheres, one of which will be our means of calculating, using language and dealing with the outside world, aind the other of which will be our path into our inner emotional natures, our dreamlands and our faculties of spatial and rhythmic apprehension.

Leaf and head, head and leaf, both are foci of reception and transmission, interfaces of exchange between hidden and invisible chemical factories and the world outside that begins from the air round bark and leaf in the one case and round skin and hair in the other, the envelopes enfolding self from not self. But that division is a delusion: can the tree be separated from the air it absorbs and releases in different forms or from the gallons of water that it draws up and then transpires to the atmosphere? Can we be considered in separation from the food we swallow, the air we breathe or the impressions we receive through our senses any more than we can be from what we excrete, exhale or speak? Furthermore, can human beings be considered viable without leaf or grass or tree, the providers of our food, our air and our most delightful impressions?

There are on earth five thousand million heads like the one that transmits these words to a pen and the one whose eyes take in what is printed on the page before it. These millions of heads are constantly collapsing into the unconsciousness of sleep or death or being borne erect on striding and sitting bodies as the earth rotates and the waves of sleep and waking follow the passage of her faces into darkness and light. The vast numbers indicate the biological success of the human species but that success is now under severe threat. According to one prediction by scientists, by the beginning of the next century, the torrid zones of the earth will be reduced to desert or near desert and close to a quarter of the earth's human population will be reduced to a state of destitution as a consequence of the destruction of the Amazonian, African and Indonesian rainforests. It is no wonder that the Green Man is returning at a time of such danger to his domains.

He comes back to warn but also to help. He sums up in himself the union that ought to be maintained between humanity and Nature. In himself he is a symbol of hope: he affirms that the wisdom of man can be allied to the instinctive and emotional forces of Nature. Perhaps also he comes to

135 *Dartmoor*. Holne Chase Wood: one of the most ancient woods in Great Britain.

136 The Green Man dish
(1986) by Alan Caiger-
Smith.

help in another way. Ecology has taught us about the interdependence of
living things: the great task of exploration that faces all enquirers into the
new is the nature of consciousness, through the study of which we may
learn something of the interdependence of human minds.

When archetypes return, they bring back the memory of all their past:
the Green Man gives us again the mystery of the northern woods, the ecstatic
joy and release of the Dionysiac festivities, the gratitude for the return of
spring and the fullness of harvest, the creative spirit of the Gothic masters
and the exuberance of Renaissance artists and sculptors. In his aspect as
the Green Man of Knowledge he also faces us with impossible tasks, for

example, the task of how to live in fruitful interchange with the environment. All these are strands awaiting the scientists and poets of the future for deeper and fresh interpretations of the Green Man's inexhaustible meanings. There also await us from his past of myth, the themes of sacrifice and renewal which we have to express in new words and symbols; and to do that we have to ask, 'What is the Green Man in ourselves?'

'Man shall not live by bread alone but by every word that proceedeth out of the mouth of God.'[14] The sacrifice may be that we have to lose our sense of separateness, our being trapped within the small individual consciousness of the physical skull, before we start to live within the greater consciousness that includes and is beyond the interdependence of all human minds past, present and to come. One image for the human head — which links with the Arthurian associations of the Green Man — is that it is the Grail or Chalice that we carry on our shoulders so that it may be filled with the waters of consciousness of the Divine Self. Another image is that man is the witness, the observer, the watcher — not the maker, the changer, the doer — and that our universe came into existence in its particular form so that its glories could be seen and enjoyed and so that God could look on his works through our unclouded eyes. The Green Man, watcher and transmitter of life, is a perfect symbol of this process. If we take this image to look inwards, then we see the dark garden of the imagination woken up by the rays of the sun of consciousness. That dawn sets in train the process of psychic photosynthesis through which the symbols of the soul are renewed and flourish. If we take it to look outwards, then we see ourselves as part of the huge surface of the earth, the many-million eyed face that looks out into the solar system and the galaxies as the witness of creation.

The Green Man utters life through his mouth. His words are leaves, the living force of experience. Anciently he was the prophet: now he comes back as the archetype of the Poet, to redeem our thought and our language, to give simplicity and clarity to the confusion and complexity of modern technological society, and to point us towards renewing the harmony and the unity to the world of Nature with inescapable love.

The Green Man offers us a new understanding of the relationship between the macrocosm — the universal world — and the microcosm in ouselves. On the macrocosmic scale he symbolizes the point at which the creative power in eternity is made manifest in space and time. Hildegard of Bingen gave a special name to the manifestation of cosmic energies: *viriditas*, greenness. On the scale of the human individual *viriditas* is the operation of the Divine Word penetrating the soul and the whole body.[15] Her idea has a modern parallel in the conception, much discussed by physicists, of the Anthropic Principle, the theory that intelligence is built into the form of the universe and that the reality of the universe is tied to us and depends on us as observers.[16] It is a theory that may help us to conceive the new scale on which to think of the Green Man.

On this scale the Green Man is the mouthpiece of the inspiration of the Divine Imagination. In art and science we express and explore the works of the Divine Imagination through our own imaginations. Coleridge said that it is characteristic of the imagination that it should find unity in the many: imagination 'is the mind's approach to self-knowledge'[17] which we attain through the stepping stones of metaphor and great symbols such as the Green

Man. The Green Man is the threshold of the imagination between our outer natures and our deepest selves and, as he is so closely connected with the Great Goddess, we must also ask, 'What is the Great Goddess in ourselves?' In ancient teachings she is Sophia or Wisdom, the wisdom we so sorely need and which the Green Man is waiting to transmit to us.

In tracing the story of the Green Man we saw how he first appeared at the end of one period of the experience of humanity, that of participation in Nature, a barely conscious union of the spirit with the world of vegetation. It was a world of deep kinship with trees and woods, to which people felt as close as to their own families and tribes. The Green Man then adapted to the changing attitude to Nature of the onlooker awareness brought about by the growth of western science and technology. This stage of awareness, noble in its isolation, lonely in its nobility, is reaching the end of its dominance. Now, perhaps, the Green Man signifies the coming together of the two modes of awareness in a new experience of conscious participation, one that will bring into being a science that works in accord with the spirit and laws of Nature and an art, deepened by the objectivity of science, that escapes from the expression of private experience to utter truths, sounds and images founded in a shared and universal joy.

Our remote ancestors said to their mother Earth: 'We are yours.'

Modern humanity has said to Nature: 'You are mine.'

The Green Man has returned as the living face of the whole earth so that through his mouth we may say to the universe: 'We are one.'

137 *St-Bertrand de Comminges*. The Lady hands the Seeker a branch of the Tree of Life. A misericord carving, 1535.

Notes

Prelude

1 This Jack in the Green celebration is now an annual event at Hastings. A similar event takes place at Rochester.
2 This is based on a story told to Hamish Henderson by Geordie Stewart, who was of tinker stock, in Aberdeen in 1954. See Henderson (1958) pp. 47-85.
3 The account of the Cowdray entertainment is in Breight (1984), pp.160-3.
4 Only when I had written much of the poem did I realize that the trees as they fell into different parts of the poem were following the tree calendar on which the Celtic alphabet was based with the trees grouped according to the lunar months. See Graves (1961), pp.165-88.

Chapter 1

1 Anderson (1985).
2 See chiefly Wegner (1935) and Basford (1978).
3 See Voyce (1967), p.321.
4 Raglan (1939).
5 Ibid., p.50.
6 Ibid., p.54.
7 Seward (1933-4) and Cave (1932).
8 Ralph of Coggeshall (1875), pp.117-18.
9 See Nicholson (1959), pp.84-5.
10 See Neumann (1955), pp.18-23.
11 Quoted in Koestler (1964), p.118.
12 James (1966), p.280.
13 Rig-Veda, I. 24, 7 and X. 82, 5.
14 Transl. Swami Prabhavanda and Christopher Isherwood (1947), p.146.
15 See Gupta (1965).
16 Van Gennep (1949), Vol.I.iv, *Les cérémonies périodiques, cycliques et saisonnires*, pp.1488-1502.
17 Frazer (1900), Vol.II, pp.60-1.
18 Weber-Kellerman (1958), pp.366-85.
19 Fricker (1949), pp.7-9.
20 Jacq (1980), p.155.
21 See Price (1901) and Anderson (1971), pp.19-20.
22 James (1966), p.277.
23 See Gaignebet and Lajoux (1985), p.70, for an illustration of this carving. See also Frazer (1911), Part I (ii), p.74, for an account of the May singers of Thann who accompany a girl called the Little May Rose. She carries a garlanded hawthorn.
24 Frazer (1911), Part II (ii), pp.75-6.
25 See Morgan (1989), pp.41-52.
26 Stewart (1977), pp.62-71.
27 See Foster and Tudor-Craig (1986), p.32.
28 Ibid. See also Jacobus de Voragine (1900), Vol.III, pp.125-34.
29 Jairazhbhoy (1966), p.194.
30 See Wiles (1981).
31 See Gaignebet and Lajoux (1985), p.185.
32 Ibid., p.186.
33 See Henderson (1958), pp. 47–85.
34 See Gantz (1981), pp. 221–55.
35 See also *The Pearl Poet: his complete works*, transl. and introduction by Margaret Williams, RSCJ (paperback 1970), New York, p.50.
36 See Gascoigne (1910), Vol.II, 'The princely pleasures at Kenelworth Castle', pp.96-102.
37 Ralph of Coggeshall (1875), pp.118-20.
38 Douglas (1916), p. 104.
39 Frazer (1900), Vol.II, p.66.
40 Liturgical preface appointed for Passiontide in the Roman Missal.
41 *Enarratio in Psalmum XCIX*, PL 37, col.1272.
42 2 Sam. 5: 24.
43 See Lannoy (1971), p.xxv, and also the frontispiece which shows a Moghul painting of the Speaking Tree, *c.*1650, now in the Islamisches Museum, Berlin.

44 Steele (1894), pp.159-70.

Chapter 2

1 See Dames (1976) and (1977).
2 Gimbutas (1982), p.220.
3 *Bacchae*, 100-1.
4 See Basford (1978), p.10.
5 For discussions of Tammuz see James (1966), pp.8f., 10f. and 65f.
6 Ibid., p.14f.
7 Ovid, *Metamorphoses*, X, 476-739.
8 See Plutarch, *De Iside et Osiride* (1936), Vol.5, pp.351-83, and, for the later influence of the cult , James (1966), Ferguson (1970) and Godwin (1981).
9 See Neumann (1955), p.312.
10 *The Golden Ass*, transl. Robert Graves (paperback 1950), Harmondsworth, p.271.
11 See Neumann (1955), p.320.
12 See Ovid, *Metamorphoses*, X, 104. For aspects of the cult see James (1966), Ferguson (1970) and Godwin (1981).
13 See James (1966), pp.275-87.
14 See Kerényi (1951 and 1976).
15 Godwin (1981), p.133.
16 Plutarch (1945), *Consolatio ad uxorem*, X, Vol.VII, pp.608f.
17 His name appears in only one inscription with the first letter missing. It is a generally agreed convention that this letter should be C.
18 Ross (1987), p.62 and illus.23.
19 Klindt-Jensen (1979), pp.48-50.
20 Hatt (1970), pp.245-6 and 271.
21 See Campbell (1974), p.412.
22 Sheridan and Ross (1975), p.15.
23 See the article by David Keys, 'Heads of stone cast new light on Celtic cult', *The Independent*, 30 May 1988, p.6.
24 *The Mabinogion*; see Gantz (1976), pp.79-81.
25 Ovid, *Metamorphoses*, X, 642f.
26 Vitruvius, ed. Granger (1931), Vol.II, pp.104-5.
27 Toynbee and Ward-Perkins (1950).
28 Vitruvius, ed. Granger (1931), Vol.I, pp.208-9.
29 See von Mercklin (1962), pp.147-92 and numerous illustrations.
30 James (1966), pp.161-2.
31 *The Shepherd of Hermas*, transl. Charles H.Hoole (1870), London, 8th similitude, pp.110-23.

32 See Mendel (1914), Vol.2, pp.546-9.
33 See von Massow (1932) and Wightman (1970).
34 See the account in Basford (1978), pp.10-11 and the references given there.
35 Kempf (1964).

Chapter 3

1 See Gaignebet and Lajoux (1985), p.76.
2 White (1968), p.84.
3 See White (1962).
4 White (1968), p.84.
5 Ibid. p.84.
6 Mâle (1950), p.57.
7 Ibid.
8 Ibid.
9 Anderson (1971), pp.17-18.
10 See Greenaway (1955), pp.27-8.
11 See Tom Greeves, 'Woodhenge echoes' in *PULP* (Common Ground 1989), London, p.43.
12 Transl. Lady Gregory (1973), p.46.
13 See Eph. 1: 21; 3: 10; 6: 12 and Col. 1: 16; 2: 15, 18, 20.
14 *Convivio*, II. iv, 6-8.
15 Bonser (1932), p.55.
16 Tolstoy (1988), pp.97-8.
17 Anglo-Saxon Chronicle, transl. James Ingram (1917), London, pp.201-2.
18 *De divisione naturae, PL* 122, col.732.
19 Ibid., col.733.
20 Ibid., col.833.
21 Henry (1940), p.133.
22 Basford (1978), p.12 and plates 13 and 14.
23 Ross (1967), pp.109-10.
24 Doble (1927). A fuller Breton version of the story is given in Baring-Gould and Fisher (1911), Vol.II, pp.467-73.
25 Frazer (1900), pp.257-61.

Chapter 4

1 Artashenko and Collins (1985), p.158.
2 *PL* 112, col.1037. See also Basford (1978), p.12.
3 See Lasko (1972), p.11 and plate 108, for these candlesticks.
4 Weir and Jerman (1986), p.150.
5 Ross and Sheridan (1979), p.66.
6 Weir and Jerman (1986), plate 14.
7 Dames (1976), pp. 147-8.

8 See Anderson (1985), p.21.

9 See Begg (1985), pp.61-8 and 212-14, and for many other examples.

10 Basford (1978), p.13.

11 See Pettazoni (1946).

12 Davy (1977), p.154-5.

13 Warner (1989), p.19.

14 See Jacobus de Voragine (1900), Vol.1, pp.180-1.

15 *Diwani Shamsi Tabrizi*, XI, transl. R.A. Nicholson (1952), pp.47-9.

16 See Corbin (1969), pp.53-67, and also Jung (1986), pp. 75-81.

17 Jacq (1980), pp.200-1.

18 See Bernard Sylvester, ed. Barach and Wrobel (1876).

19 *Anticlaudianus*, I. 328, *PL* 210, col.493.

20 Ibid., IX. 413, *PL* 210, col. 574.

Chapter 5

1 Basford (1978), pp.15-16. There is, for example, no mention of them in Katzenellenbogen (1951).

2 It is illustrated in Crosby *et al.* (1981), plate 9a.

3 Panofsky (1955), pp.146-68.

4 Personal communication from Malcolm Miller.

5 See Basford (1978), plate 31c.

6 See Behling (1964) on Rheims, pp.64-82.

7 See Hahnloser (1935), pp.25-6 and plates 10 and 43.

8 *Liber divinorum operum*, Visio II *PL* 197, cols.741-4. The illumination from which my description is drawn is illustrated in Jung (1953), fig.195, from a twelfth-century manuscript in the Biblioteca Governativa, Lucca, Codex 1942.

9 Behling (1964), plates LVIII and LIX.

10 See Reeves (1976), plate 4 and p.19.

11 *Paradiso*, XXVII. 109-20.

12 See the many examples in Behling (1964).

13 *De arca Noe morali*, Prol., *PL* 176, cols 617-19.

14 Adam of St Victor, *PL* 196, cols 1433-4.

15 *Paradiso*, XXVI. 64-6. The translation is by Laurence Binyon.

16 See Jacobus de Voragine (1900), Vol.3, pp.100-1.

17 See Behling (1964), plate CVII.

18 Basford (1978), plate 52b.

19 See Canseliet (1984).

20 *Liber divinorum operum*, Visio X xix *PL* 197, col. 1021.

21 See Ernst Levy in von Simson (1956), pp.235-59.

Chapter 6

1 Such as the story of Conchubar told in the *Book of Leinster*. Conchubar, seeing the changes in creation and the eclipses of the sun and moon, asked a druid what these changes meant. The druid answered that it was because Jesus Christ, the Son of God, was being crucified at that very time. W.B. Yeats gives the full story as a note to 'The Secret Rose' in *Collected Poems* (1950), London, pp.527-8.

2 See Backman (1952), p.67.

3 Adhémar (1936), pp.224-32.

4 Hahnloser (1935), p.25.

5 See Boeck (1960), p.36f.

6 Duby (1970), p.352.

7 The original statue is now in the Kulturhistorisches Museum, Magdeburg.

8 Anderson (1985), p.103.

9 See Highfield (1953).

10 See Basford (1978), p.123, and Pevsner (revised Bridget Cherry, 1975), *Wiltshire*, Harmondsworth, pp.402-3.

11 *Purgatorio*, XXIX. 42.

12 See Eberly (1989).

13 Basford (1978), p.19.

14 See the account of the chapel by Christopher Wilson in McWilliam (1978), pp.409-17.

15 1 Esd. 3: 12.

16 See Dames (1977), pp.162-3.

17 There is, of course, the example quoted earlier (see p.66 and fig. 46) of the woman on the font at Winterbourne Monkton giving birth to leaves.

Chapter 7

1 Reproduced in Dickens (1966), fig.39.

2 Bishop Latimer, *Sermons*, (Everyman edn 1906), London, pp.179-80.

3 Stubbes, ed. Furnivall (1877-9), Part I, p.149.

4 See the many examples to be found in Johnson (1929) and McKevrow and Ferguson (1932).

5 Signorini (1976) pp.205–12.

167

6 For these friezes see Hartt (1969), p.180.

7 See Serlio (1964), Book IV, pp.191-9.

8 Such as those to be seen on the portal of the Jesuit Church in Arles, now the Musée de l'Art Chrétien, or in the choirstalls of Moissac.

9 *Merry Wives*, IV. iii. 29-35.

10 *The Old Wives' Tale*, Peele (1970), p.415.

11 *David and Bethsabe*, lines 1455-6. See Peele (1970), p.239.

12 See Wiles (1981), pp.7-30.

13 *The Minor English Poems of John Milton*, ed. H.C. Beeching (1903), p.8.

14 'The Garden', lines 47-8.

15 'Upon Appleton House, to my Lord Fairfax', lines 695-6.

16 Ibid., lines 481-4.

17 Ibid., lines 577-84.

18 Ibid., lines 585-92.

19 Ibid., lines 609-16.

20 'The Garden', lines 43-4.

21 Vaughan wrote this in a letter to his cousin John Aubrey, who had enquired of him about the traditions of the Welsh bards. See Vaughan, ed. Martin (1957), Vol.II, pp.696-7.

22 See Wiles (1981), p.55.

23 The original Green Man has recently been replaced by an excellent replica in the restoration of the gates.

24 See Judge (1979).

25 I am indebted to my kind correspondent Suzanne Valadon for this information.

Chapter 8

1 *The Crock of Gold*, London (1912), pp.191-2.

2 See Vernadsky (1929).

3 Lovelock (1987), p.x.

4 See Anderson (1988), p.179.

5 Ibid., fig.89.

6 Ibid., fig.94.

7 Ibid., fig.120.

8 Ibid, fig.70.

9 See Common Ground (1989).

10 As, for example, in his didactic poem *Die Metamorphose der Pflanzen*.

11 See *The Theory of Life* in *Selected Poetry and Prose of Samuel Taylor Coleridge*, ed. D. Stauffer (1951), New York, and also Barfield (1971), pp.41-58.

12 *Lamia*, II. 229-36.

13 *The Prelude*, II. 213-14.

14 Matt. 4: 4.

15 *Liber divinorum operum*, Visio IV. xxi, *PL* 197, col.813.

16 See Barrow and Tipler (1986).

17 Barfield (1971), p.117.

Bibliography

Abbreviation PL stands for *Patrologia Latina*, ed. J.P. Migne (1844-68), Paris

ADHÉMAR, Jean (1936) 'La Fontaine de Saint-Denis,' *Revue Archéologique*, I, pp. 224-32

ALAN OF LILLE (1973) *Anticlaudianus or The Good and Perfect Man*, transl. James Sheridan, Toronto

ANDERSON, M.D. (1971) *History and Imagery in British Churches*, London

ANDERSON, William (1983) *Holy Places of the British Isles*, London

— (1985) *The Rise of the Gothic*, London and Boston

— (1989) 'The Green Man', *Parabola*, XIV, 3, pp.26-33

— (1989) 'The Green Man', *Pulp* (Common Ground), London, p.25

ATROSHENKO, V.I. and Collins, Judith (1985) *The Origins of the Romanesque: Near-Eastern influences on European art 4th-12th centuries*, London

BACKMAN, E.Louis (1952) *Religious Dances in the Christian Church and in Popular Medicine*, transl. E.Classen, London

BARFIELD, Owen (1971) *What Coleridge Thought*, Oxford

BARROW, John D. and Tipler, Frank J. (1986) *The Anthropic Cosmological Principle*, Oxford

BARING-GOULD, Sabine and Fisher, John (1907-13) *The Lives of the British Saints*, 4 vols, London

BASFORD, Kathleen (1978) *The Green Man*, Ipswich

BEGG, Ean (1985) *The Cult of the Black Virgin*, London

BEHLING, Lottlisa (1964) *Die Pflanzenwelt der mittelalterlichen Kathedrälen*, Cologne

BERNARD, Sylvester (1876) *De mundi universitate*, ed. C.S. Barach and J. Wrobel, Innsbruck

BERNHEIMER, R. (1952) *Wild Men in the Middle Ages: a study in art, sentiment, and demonology*, Cambridge, Mass.

BOECK, W. (1960) *Der Bamberger Meister*, Tübingen

BONSER, Wilfrid (1932) 'Survivals of paganism in Anglo-Saxon England,' *Birmingham and Midland Archaeological Society Transactions and Proceedings*, LVI, pp.37-70

— (1961) *A Bibliography of Folklore as contained in the first eighty years of the publications of the Folklore Society(1878-1957)* (published for the Folklore Society), London

BREIGHT, Curtis Charles (1989) 'Caressing the great: Viscount Montague's entertainment of Elizabeth at Cowdray, 1591', *Sussex Archaeological Collections*, 127, pp. 147-66

CAMPBELL, Joseph (1974) *Creative Mythology: the masks of God*, London

CANSELIET, Eugène (1984) 'Les écoinçons des stalles de la cathédrale de Poitiers et leur inteprétation alchimique', *Atlantis*, 332, pp.291-308

CARTER, R.O.M. and H.M. (1967) 'The foliate head in England', *Folklore*, 78, pp.269-74

CARY, George (1956) *The Medieval Alexander*, ed. D.J.A. Ross, Cambridge

CAVE, C.J.P. (1932) 'The roof bosses in Ely Cathedral', *Proceedings and Communications of the Cambridge Antiquarian Society*, 32, pp.33-46

— (1947) 'Jack in the Green carvings', letter in *Country Life*, 4 July 1947

— (1948) *Roof Bosses in Medieval Churches*, Cambridge

— (1953) *Medieval carvings in Exeter Cathedral*, Harmondsworth

CHAMBERS, Sir E.K. (1903) *The Medieval Stage*, 2 vols, Oxford

CHASTEL, André (1954) *Marsile Ficin et l'art*, Geneva and Lille

CHILD, F.J. (1882-98) *The English and Scottish Popular Ballads*, 5 vols, Boston

Common Ground (1989) *Pulp*, London

CORBIN, Henry (1969) *Creative Imagination in the Sufism of Ibn 'Arabi*, transl. Ralph Manheim, London

CROSBY, Sumner McKnight, Hayward, Jane, Little, Charles T. and Wixom, William D. (1981) *The Royal Abbey of Saint-Denis in the Time of Abbot Suger 1122-1151* (Metropolitan Museum of Art catalogue), New York

DAMES, Michael (1976) *The Silbury Treasure: the Great Goddess rediscovered*, London and New York

DAVY, Marie-Madeleine (1977) *Initiation à la symbolique romane (XIIe sicle)*, Paris

DICKENS, A.G. (1966) *Reformation and Society in Sixteenth-Century Europe*, London

DOBLE, Revd Gilbert (1927) *Saint Melor: a Cornish saint*, Cornish Saints Series 13, Shipston- on-Stour

DOUGLAS, Norman (1916) *London Street Games*, London

DUBY, Georges (1976) *Le Temps des cathédrales: l'art et la societé 980-1420* (new edn), Paris

EBERLY, Susan S. (1989) 'A thorn among the lilies: the hawthorn in medieval love allegory', *Folklore*, 100, 1, pp. 41-52

FERGUSON, John (1970) *The Religions of the Roman Empire*, London and New York

FRAZER, Sir J. G. (1890-1915) *The Golden Bough*, 12 vols, London

FOSTER, Richard and Tudor-Craig, Pamela (1986) *The Secret Life of Paintings*, Woodbridge

FOWLER, James (1873) 'On medieval representations of the months and the seasons', *Archaeologia*, 44, pp. 137–89

FRICKER, Robert (1949) 'The Vogel Gryff Pageant', *Journal of the International Folk Music Council*, I, pp.7-8

GAIGNEBET, Claude and Lajoux, Jean-Dominique (1985) *Art profane et religion populaire au moyen âge*, Paris

GANTZ, Jeffrey, transl. (1976) *The Mabinogion*, Harmondsworth

— (1981) *Early Irish Myths, and Sagas*, Harmondsworth

GASCOIGNE, George (1910) *The Complete Works*, ed. John W. Cunliffe, 2 vols, Cambridge

GENNEP, Arnold van (1943-66) *Manuel de folklore français contemporain*, 6 parts, Paris

GIMBUTAS, Mariya (1982) *The Goddesses and Gods of Old Europe 6500-3500 BC: myths and cult images* (new edn), London and New York

— (1989) *The Language of the Goddess*, San Francisco

GIREL, Louis (1945) 'La fête du feuillu à Versoix', *Folklore Suisse*, 1, p. 394

GLUECK, Nelson (1966) *Deities and Dolphins: the story of the Nabataeans*, London

GODWIN, Joscelyn (1981) *Mystery Religions in the Ancient World*, London and New York

GRAVES, Robert (1955) *Myths of the Greeks and Romans*, 2 vols, Harmondsworth

—— (1961) *The White Goddess: a historical grammar of poetic myth* (amended and enlarged edn), London

GREENAWAY, George William (1955) *Saint Boniface*, London

GREENE, Robert (1911) *A Pleasant Conceited Comedy of George a Greene, The Pinner of Wakefield* (Malone Reprints), London

GREGORY, Lady (1973) *The voyages of St Brendan the Navigator and stories of the saints of Ireland, forming a book of saints and wonders* (republished), Gerrards Cross

GUPTA, Sankar Sen, ed. (1965) *Tree Symbol Worship in India*, Calcutta

HAHNLOSER, Hans R. (1935) *Villard de Honnecourt: Kritische Gesamtausgabe des Bauhüttenbuches ms.fr19093 der Pariser Nationalbibliothek*, Vienna

HARTT, Frederick (1979) *Michelangelo: the complete sculptures*, London

HATT, Jean-Jacques (1970) *Celts and Gallo-Romans*, transl. James Hogarth, London

HENDERSON, Hamish (1958) 'The Green Man of knowledge', *Scottish Studies* 2(1), pp. 47–85

HENRY, Françoise (1940) *Irish Art in the Early Christian Period*, London

HIGHFIELD, J.R.L. (1953) 'The Green Squire', *Medium Aevum*, XXII, pp.18-23

HOLE, Christina (1940) *English Folklore*, London

— (1952) *English Custom and Usage*, London

— (1975) *British Folklore Customs*, London

HOLT, J.C. (1983) *Robin Hood*, London and New York

HOPPER, Vincent (1969) *Medieval Number Symbolism: its sources, meaning, and influence on thought and expression* (republished), New York

JACOBUS DE VORAGINE (1900) *The Golden Legend or lives of the saints as Englished by William Caxton*, ed. F.S. Ellis, 7 vols, London

JACQ, Christian (1972) *Le Message spirituel de Saint-Bertrand de Comminges*, Paris

—— (1980) *Le Message des constructeurs des cathédrales*, Paris

JAIRAZBHOY, R.A. (1966) *Oriental Influence in Western Art*, Bombay and London

JAMES, E.O. (1961) *Seasonal Feasts and Festivals*, London and New York

— (1966) *The Tree of Life*, Leiden

JOHN SCOTUS ERIUGENA (1968, 1972, 1981) *Periphyseon (De divisione naturae)*, ed. J.P. Sheldon-Williams with collaboration of Ludwig Bieler, 3 vols (Books I, II and III) (Scriptores Latini Hiberniae), Dublin

JOHNSON, Alfred Forbes (1929) *German Renaissance Title-Borders* (for the Bibliographical Society), Oxford

JUDGE, Roy (1979) *The Jack in the Green: a May Day custom*, Ipswich

JUNG, C.G. (1933) *Modern Man in Search of a Soul*, transl. W.S. Dell and Caryl S. Brahms, London

— (1953) *Psychology and Alchemy*, transl. R.F.C. Hull, vol.12 of *Collected Works*, London

— (1986) *Four Archetypes: mother, rebirth, spirit, trickster* (paperback), London

KATZENELLENBOGEN, Adolf (1954) *The Sculptural Programs of Chartres Cathedral*, Baltimore

KEEN, Maurice (1961) *The Outlaws of Medieval England*, London

KEMPF, Theodor Konrad (1964) 'Untersuchungen und Beobachtungen am Trierer Dom 1961-3', *Germania*, 42, pp.126-41

KENNEDY, Douglas (1940) 'Robin Hood and the Bowery', *English Dance and Song*, 4, 5, pp. 62–3

— (1940–1948) 'Jack-a-Lent,' *English Dance and Song*, 4, no. 4, pp. 42–3 and 12, no. 5, pp. 72–5

KERÉNYI, Carl (1951) *The Gods of the Greeks*, London and New York

— (1976) *Dionysus: archetypal image of indestructible life*, Princeton

KIGHTLY, Charles (1986) *The Customs and Ceremonies of Britain: an encylopaedia of living traditions*, London and New York

KLINDT-JENSEN, Ole (1979) *Gundestrup Kedelen* (Nationalmuseet), Copenhagen

KOESTLER, Arthur (1964) *The Act of Creation*, London

LANNOY, Richard (1971) *The Speaking Tree: a study of Indian culture and society*, Oxford

LIGHTBOWN, Ronald (1986) *Mantegna, with a complete catalogue of the paintings, drawings, and prints*, Oxford

LUBAC, Henri de (1954-64) *Exégèse médiévale: les quatre sens de l'écriture*, 4 vols, Paris

MCKEVROW, R.B. and Ferguson, F.S. (1932) *Title-Page Borders Used in England and Scotland 1485-1640* (for the Bibliographical Society), Oxford

MCWILLIAM, Colin (1978) *Lothian except Edinburgh* (The Buildings of Scotland), Harmondsworth

MÂLE, Emile (1913) *Religious Art in France: XIII century*, transl. Dora Nussey, London

— (1950) *La Fin du paganisme en Gaule et les plus anciennes basiliques chrétiennes*, Paris

MASSOW, Wilhelm von (1932) *Die Grabmälen von Neumagen*, Berlin and Leipzig

MENDEL, Gustave (1912-14) *Musees impériaux ottomans: catalogue des sculptures grecques, romaines, et byzantines*, 2 vols, Istanbul

MERCKLIN, Eugen von (1962) *Antike Figuralkapitelle,* Deutsches Archäologisches Institut, Berlin

MORGAN, Gareth (1989) 'Mummers and Momoeri', *Folklore*, 100, 1, pp. 84-7

NEUMANN, Erich (1955) *The Great Mother: an analysis of the archetype*, transl. Ralph Manheim, London

NICHOLSON, Irene (1959) *Firefly in the Night: a study of ancient Mexican poetry and symbolism*, London

OVID (1916) *Metamorphoses*, ed. F.J. Miller (Loeb edn), 2 vols, London and Cambridge, Mass.

PANOFSKY, Erwin (1955) *Meaning in the Visual Arts*, New York

PEELE, George (1970) *Life and Works*, 3 vols, New Haven and London

PETTAZZONI, R. (1946) 'The pagan origins of the three-headed representation of the Christian Trinity', *Journal of the Warburg and Courtauld Institutes*, 9, pp.135-51

PEVSNER, Sir Nikolaus (1945) *The Leaves of Southwell*, Harmondsworth

— (1951-74) *The Buildings of England* series, Harmondsworth

PHILLIPS, G.L. (1949) 'May Day is Sweeps' Day', *Folklore*, 60, 1, pp.217-25

PLUTARCH (1927–67) *Moralia*, Loeb edn, 14 vols, London

PORTEOUS, A. (1928) *Forest Folklore, Mythology and Romance*, London

PORTER, Enid (1974) *The Folklore of East Anglia*, London

PRICE, C.E. (1901) *The Roodscreen of the Parish Church of Charlton-on-Otmoor*, Oxford Archaeological Society reprint no.18, 1901

RAGLAN, Lady (1939) 'The Green Man in church architecture', *Folklore*, 50, 1, pp.45-57

REEVES, Marjorie (1976) *Joachim of Fiore and the Prophetic Future*, London

REMNANT, G.L. (1969) *A catalogue of Misericords in Great Britain*, with an essay by M. D. Anderson, Oxford

ROBINS, R. (1951) 'Some notes on the Green Man in Germany', *English Dance and Song*, 15, 6, pp. 181–2

ROSS, Anne (1967) *Pagan Celtic Britain: studies in iconography and tradition*, London (See also Sheridan and Ross)

RUMI, Jalalu'ddin (1898) *Selected Poems from the Diwani Shamsi Tabrizi*, ed. and transl. Reynold A. Nicholson, Cambridge

SCHAPIRO, Meyer (1985) *The Sculpture of Moissac*, London and New York

SERLIO, Sebastiano (1964) *Tutte l'opere d'architettura e prospetiva* (reprint of original edn, Vicenza 1618), Ridgewood, New Jersey

SEWARD, Sir A.C. (1933-4) 'The foliage, flowers and fruit of Southwell Chapter House,' *Proceedings of the Cambridge Antiquarian Society*, 35, pp.1-32

SHARPE, Cecil (1916) *One Hundred English Folksongs*, London

SHERIDAN, Ronald and Ross, Anne (1975) *Grotesques and Gargoyles in the Medieval Church*, Newton Abbot

SIGNORINI, Rodolfo (1976) 'L'autoritratto del Mantegna nella Camera degli Sposi', *Mitteilungen des Kunsthistorisches Institut in Florenz* 20, pp.205–12

SIMSON, Otto von (1956) *The Gothic Cathedral: the origins of Gothic architecture and the medieval concept of order*, London

SMITH, J.C.D. (1969) *Church Woodcarvings: a West Country study*, Newton Abbot

— (1974) *A Guide to Church Woodcarvings*, Newton Abbot

SPEIRS, John (1949) 'Sir Gawain and the Green Knight,' *Scrutiny*, XVI, 4, pp.274-300

STEELE, Robert (1894) *The Story of Alexander retold from the originals*, London

STEWART, Bob (1977) *Where is Saint George? Pagan imagery in English folksong*, Bradford-on-Avon

STRUTT, J. (1801) *Sports and Pastimes of the People of England*, London

STUBBES, Philip (1877-9) *Anatomy of Abuses*, ed. Frederick J. Furnivall (for the New Shakespeare Society), Part I

TOLSTOY, Nikolai (1985) *The Quest for Merlin*, London

TOYNBEE, J.M.C. (1962) *Art in Roman Britain*, London

— (1964) *Art in Britain under the Romans*, London

TOYNBEE, J.M.C. and Ward-Perkins, J.B. (1950) 'Peopled scrolls: a Hellenistic motif in Imperial art', *Papers of the British School at Rome*, XVIII (New Series, Vol.IV), pp.1-43

TRENOW, Dave (1973) 'The Green Man', *English Folk Dance and Song*, 35, 3, pp. 96–7

VAUGHAN, Henry (1957) *The Works of Henry Vaughan*, ed. L.C. Martin, Oxford

VERNADSKY, Vladimir (1929) *La Biosphère*, Paris

VITRUVIUS (1931) *De Architectura*, ed. and transl. Frank Granger (Loeb edn), 2 vols, London and Cambridge, Mass.

VOYCE, Arthur (1967) *The Art and Architecture of Medieval Russia*, Norman, Oklahoma

WARNER, Marina (1976) *Alone of All her Sex: the myth and cult of the Virgin Mary*, London

— (1989) 'Signs of the fifth element' in *The Tree of Life: new images of an ancient symbol* (catalogue of Common Ground Exhibition, South Bank Centre), London, pp.7-47

WATTS, Alan (1983) *Myth and Ritual in Christianity* (paperback), London

WEBER-KELLERMAN, I. (1958) 'Laubkönig und Schössmeier: Geschichte und Deutung pfingstlichter Vegetationsgebräuche in Thüringen', *Deutsches Jahrbuch für Volkskunde*, IV, pp.366-85

WEGNER, Max (1935) 'Die Blattmaske' in *Das siebente Jahrzehnt: Festschrift zum 70. Geburtstag von Adolph Goldschmidt*, pp.43-50, Berlin

WEIR, Anthony and Jerman, James (1986) *Images of Lust: sexual carvings on medieval churches*, London

WHITE, Lynn, Jnr (1962) *Medieval Technology and Social Change*, Oxford

— (1968) *Dynamo and Virgin Reconsidered*, Cambridge, Mass.

WILDRIDGE, T. Tindall (1899) *The Grotesque in Church Art*, London

WIGHTMAN, Edith Mary (1970) *Roman Trier and the Treveri*, London

WILES, David (1981) *The Early Plays of Robin Hood*, Ipswich

WITHINGTON, R. (1963) *English Pageantry: an historical outline* (reprint of 1918 edn), Oxford

WOLFRAM, Richard (1932) 'Robin Hood und Hobby Horse', *Wiener Prähistorische Zeitschrft*, XIX, pp. 357–74

Index